MODELS
OF
CHRISTIAN
ETHICS

MODELS
OF
CHRISTIAN
ETHICS

By

Michael E. Allsopp

Scranton: The University of Scranton Press

Library of Congress Cataloging-in-Publication Data

Allsopp, Michael E.
    Models of Christian ethics / by Michael E. Allsopp
        p. cm.
    Includes bibliographical references and index.
    ISBN 1-58966-054-4
    1. Christian ethics. I. Title.

B1251 .A44 2002
241–dc21   2002032445

Distribution:

The University of Scranton Press
Linden & Monroe
Scranton, PA 18510
Phone: 1–800–941–3081
Fax: 1–800–941–8804

DEDICATION

For
Kathleen, Frank, Maureen, Carmel, and Patrick
who have taught me the meaning of
family and friendship

ABOUT THE AUTHOR

Michael Allsopp has taught Christian Ethics, and Biomedical Ethics at St. Patrick's College (Manly, Australia), Creighton University (Omaha, NE), and Barry University (Miami Shores, FL). He received his doctorate in theology "with highest honors" from the Gregorian University in Rome, in 1980. As well as contributions to *Irish Theological Quarterly*, *Chicago Studies*, *Humane Medicine*, *Christian Bioethics*, and *Explorations*, he is co-editor of *John Henry Newman: Theology & Reform* (1992), *Saving Beauty: Further Studies in Hopkins* (1994), and *Veritatis Splendor: American Responses* (1995). In 1999, he edited *Ethics and the Catechism of the Catholic Church* (University of Scranton Press).

CONTENTS

INTRODUCTION

Avery Dulles's groundbreaking *Models of the Church* examined theology's chief "models" of the Christian Church. After explaining the use of models (approaches, analogies) in ecclesiology, as well as their limits and possibilities in theology, Dulles looked at the way that the church has been depicted as "institution," "mystical communion," "sacrament," "herald," and "servant." In a similar way, this book now examines the major "models" of Christian ethics.

As Vincent MacNamara illustrates in *Faith & Ethics* (1985), the field of Christian ethics has gone through several periods of rapid change during its 2000 year history. However, nothing equals the changes that have been seen during the years since World War II. The past four decades have been years of questioning and renewal. Due to the influence of Anglo-American moral philosophy, the ecumenical movement, and the renewal in Biblical studies, Christian ethics has experienced unprecedented change. And with that change, new questions have arisen: What is the significance of the words *Christian*, *theological/theology*, and expressions such as *Christian ethics*, *theological ethics*, and *moral theology*? How is the indissolubility of marriage arrived at in Christian ethics? What is the source of the prohibition on taking life? What is the basis of Catholic social teaching? As MacNamara writes early in his book, "What is one to make of frequent references to the immutable laws of God? Is the appeal to the biblical themes in favor of liberation justified? What value is to be attached to the expression 'in the light of revelation' which plays some part in many official church pronouncements?"(1–2)

This is a book about method in Christian ethics. Like MacNamara's book, *Models of Christian Ethics* aims at developing intellectual rigor in religious ethics by strengthening clarity and reducing confusion. It has been written in the belief that just as no graduate in counseling psychology should be ignorant of "models" associated with Freud, Skinner, and Piaget, pastors and religious educators should not be unaware of the ethical theories associated with James Gustafson, Gustavo Gutierrez, Stanley Hauerwas, Richard McCormick, Joseph Fletcher, Jean Porter, and Sharon Welch.

This book will assist pastors, church leaders, and religious educators; it will benefit those conducting or taking college courses in morality. It will be especially useful to graduate students in ministry programs, and seminary students of all Christian traditions. While it has been written for both Protestants and Catholics, *Models of Christian Ethics* will help all serious readers to better understand how Christian ethics is being done today, to help resolve questions about the sources of Christian ethics, and to clarify the relationship between moral philosophy and moral theology. The book looks at the connections between faith and reason, context and content, laws and values, nature and grace, personal journey and physical structure, science and religion. As it describes the various "models," it deals indirectly with the relationships between stories and symbols, rights and duties, motives and outcomes, gender and nature, gift and merit, call and response, virtue and action, passivity and creativity, the community and the individual. Throughout its chapters, *Models of Christian Ethics* examines the interconnections current "models" make between Jesus and Einstein, the Bible and the Church, and conscience and magisterium.

Reading this book will not only force readers to relate authoritative statements of the past with speculative predictions of the future: It will enable them to appreciate better the exciting present of Christian ethics. Those who possess some knowledge of contemporary Anglo-American philosophy and European theology will find that this material, with which they are familiar, is handled here in new ways. The book's chapters will reacquaint them with leading Protestant and Roman Catholic ethicists whose writings have shaped the church's recent discussions on health care, economics, the environment, sexuality and marriage.

Rather than presenting one particular approach, or several brief summaries of major Protestant or Catholic theories as textbooks in Christian morality usually do, *Models of Christian Ethics* does not offer a final statement about the nature of Christian morality, but focuses throughout on providing insights into the most important "models" or "analogies." The book lets readers decide for themselves using John Henry Newman's famous motto, "*Ex umbris et imaginibus in veritatem.*"

The book's "visual aids" will permit each student to gain an easier and more lasting understanding of contemporary religious ethics. The use of "models" in Christian thought, for instance, in Avery Dulles's *Models of the Church*, or Bernard Lonergan's *Method in Theology*, have provided readers with clearer insights into the church, the sacraments, and the study of theology. The author of this book believes that using this same approach will enable readers to better understand and grasp the results of arguably the most creative and complex time in the 2000 year history of Christian ethics.

Each chapter in this book begins with an overview of a "model," and places it in its context; then, it focuses on a major book or series of essays by a significant exponent of the approach. Finally, each chapter closes with an assessment of the "model's" strengths and weaknesses, and its place in the future. The structure of these chapters will make them easier to use in college and parish courses.

The six "models" presented here have been chosen because of their importance, and their interest for the Church's future. Two other criteria have been used in making decisions about inclusion: The "model's" usefulness for those who will be shaping the future of nursing, medicine, law, politics, and business; and a "model's" ability to generate new insights for tomorrow's Christians as they engage with Jews, Muslims, Buddhists, and Hindus in seeking solutions to tomorrow's global moral questions.

This book has not been written on an island. I must thank Richard Rousseau who directs the University of Scranton Press, and Patty Mecadon, Production Manager, for their trust. I am indebted to colleagues who have read the manuscript, and to students who have provided useful comments as the work developed. I am grateful, in particular, to William P. Frost (University of Dayton), Edouard Hamel (formerly Dean of the Faculty of Theology at the Gregorian University), Charles E. Curran (Southern Methodist University), Bruce Malina (Creighton University), Gerald O'Collins (Gregorian University), John O'Grady (Barry University), Msgr. Harry Davis (Past President, St. Patrick's College, Manly), and Rev. Dr. Richard Ward (Retired Senior Pastor, United Methodist Church, Aberdeen), for their support and encouragement over the years. I also wish to thank William P. Frost, in his capacity as Editor of the journal *Explorations,* and Rev. Vincent Twomey, SVD, editor of the *Irish Theological Quarterly*, St. Patrick's College, Maynooth, for granting permission for the publication of essays that appeared in earlier forms in their journals.

Finally, I would like to dedicate this book to my brothers and sisters who have humbled me throughout my academic life by their cards, letters, gifts, and hospitality—their many enduring expressions of love and kindness: The signs of family.

Michael E. Allsopp
St. Patrick's Day, 2001

CHAPTER 1

Feminist Ethics

Feminist ethics is the most powerful movement in contemporary Christian ethics. Powered by a set of beliefs and goals that have already reshaped some of the basic assumptions and principles of the discipline, feminist ethics now has its own language, and literary style. It has its own methodological and epistemological rules. It possesses its own clear agenda. Sharing some of the features we find in situation ethics, casuistry, and liberation ethics, Christian feminism embraces a distinctive approach to moral issues—as well as a unique set of normative principles and operative rules.

Feminist Ethics: An Overview

Feminists start with critiques of ethics. For Harvard's Carol Gilligan, the best known writer on women's moral development, psychological research into moral behavior and theories of moral development have largely misunderstood women—their motives and moral commitments, their values and ethical development. Consistently, research has been built upon male observations about men's behavior.[1] Sharon Welch's highly acclaimed, *A Feminist Ethic of Risk* (1990), opens with the argument that America's rationally deduced, male-dominated nuclear weapons policies are classic examples of dangerously flawed thought; that United States foreign policy's confidence in superior economic and military strength has consistently masked immorality as ethics.[2] For a third feminist writer, Virginia L. Warren, mainstream medical ethics has used a male perspective to frame moral questions and to shape ethical solutions. As well, it has set up debates in ways that have kept women on the defensive.[3] Such ethics seduces women to work within its framework by offering hope for improvement —but only if women do not rock the patriarchal boat too vigorously (34). In Warren's view, both the way that bioethics looks at the rightness of actions, and how bioethics is done—the process—exhibit male biases and masculine distortions (35).

These criticisms of ethics are central to Eleanor Humes Haney's summary review of feminist critiques of Catholic and Protestant moral theology. What has been called "Judeo-Christian ethics" represents only a part of Christian and human experience—that of men. These men were usually called to celibacy rather than to marriage, to positions of power rather than to service, and to lives as insiders in societies rather than existences on the margin, according to Haney.[4] "Little of the ethics considered significant by the church and by divinity schools has been written by women, by non-whites, by the poor, and by those whose expressed sexual orientations deviated from a heterosexual and marital one" (115).

Because of its "parochialism" and its "arrogance," feminists have never felt comfortable doing Christian ethics as it has been done. However, they have also seen that they could not simply fill in history's gaps, or add women's experiences to the historical record. "For women to go back to some starting point in the past or to some already defined authority is to do little more than think men's thoughts after them," Haney explains (116). From the start, feminist ethics sought to articulate and make real the visions of women—and men—who shared beliefs and values grounded in women's authentic experience of the "right" and their communal apprehension of the "good." Here we see the basis for the claim that Christian feminist ethics relates to traditional Christian ethics as critique and alternative (122).

Today, 30 years after Betty Friedan's *Feminine Mystique* (1963), Kate Millett's *Sexual Politics* (1970), Mary Daly's *Radical Feminism* (1973), and Rosemary Radford Ruether's *New Woman/New Earth* (1975), there is obvious pluralism within feminist ethics. "Feminists have understandable reasons both to reject and to promote belief in a common or universal morality," Margaret Farley says.[5] Black feminist liberation ethics has its own distinctive emphases.[6] However, there are some generally shared methodological principles, common goals, and characteristic emphases within the movement. The two original streams, one focused on caring, the other on justice, have been brought together by recent feminist writers, Peta Bowden, and Rita C. Manning.[7] The initial insights into human knowledge and decision-making have been developed and strengthened; feminists have actively applied their analyses to areas of life vital to women. Looking at this model of Christian ethics, examining its roots, and assessing its strengths for the future will be the aim of this chapter.

From the start, feminists have been critical of mainstream moral theories because of a number of observed flaws in their methods.[8] In Susan Sherwin's judgment, both feminist ethics and medical ethics share a sense of frustration about the level of abstraction and generalization that one finds in mainstream work in bioethics.[9] To correct this, woman-ists have been committed to including contextual details in their analyses, and for making space for personal aspects of relationships in their moral decision making (21–22). "A feminine consciousness regards the *gender* traits that have been traditionally associated with women—in particular, nurturance, compassion, caring—as positive *human* traits," Rosemarie Tong explains.[10] Feminist philosophers have stressed the particularity and embodiment of all visions; they have supported the conviction that human knowledge is personal and drawn from situated perspectives. Consequently, they have affirmed the belief that all knowledge is essentially partial.

The focus on connectedness and context—the central insight in situation ethics—makes evident other conclusions: The nature of specific relationships is an important element of ethical analysis; an ethics of actions is incomplete when evaluation is done in abstraction from the relationships that exist between the participants and those affected; objective and accurate knowledge results from a patchwork of inherently incomplete perspectives. Further, "Within feminist ethics, there is widespread criticism of the assumption that the role of ethics is to clarify obligations among individuals who are viewed as paradigm-atically equal, independent, rational, and autonomous," Sherwin writes (21).

Besides the twin emphasis on the contextuality of knowledge, and the moral significance of specific, unequal relationships, feminist writers have enlarged the discussion of morality in other important ways. From the start, they have broadened the scope of ethics; they have focused attention on "housekeeping" issues, on wildlife, pets, and the environment—subjects on the margins of mainstream ethics. Eco-feminists have proposed new images of creation, and reformulations of the relationships between God, humans, and the non-human world.[11] Feminists have been influential in biomedical ethics.[12] They have looked at how women deal with death and dying, and found that mothers, wives, daughters, and companions deal with these events in ways that are quite different from men of both dominant and non-dominant cultures.[13] They have developed theories of disability; they have reexamined the moral significance of birth, sex selection, surrogacy, and ectogenesis. Womanists have challenged liberal societies to reshape their social structures in ways that deal more justly with the family.[14]

The body plays a significant role in a number of feminist analyses—but one finds little support for classic "natural law" morality. They have been critical of theories that equate ethics with decision making. Further, feminists have argued that ethics should be concerned not only with actions and relationships, but also with questions of character and the development of attitudes of trust within relationships, a theme that has special significance for Annette Baier.[15] Feminists have rejected the view of human persons as "self-isolating," and insisted on the need for "a corrective to a liberal philosophy that fails to understand persons as embodied subjects, with essential capacity and need for union with other persons," Margaret Farley states.[16] Rather than a focus on rational self-interest (Ayn Rand), or on the patterns and potentialities inherent in human nature (Grisez), womanists have set their sights on developing a social ethics whose final goal is the liberation of oppressed groups from structural injustice.

A number of features are characteristic of feminist ethical theories of decision making in the 1990s. First, in place of a Kantian conception of rationality (seen as a now discredited device for claiming mastery and control, as well as for refusing to acknowledge the legitimacy of differing perspectives and different relations to life and nature), womanists advocate wholism in the process of moral discernment. Second, there is "a firm methodological commitment to maintaining a focus on the experience of women as the primary source for feminist ethics" (Farley, 230). As well, women have opted for the familiar rather than the distanced, for building upon the insights of Virginia Woolf, Maria Montessori, and research into women's ways of death, speech, work, and management. Women writers have chosen to articulate ethics in distinctly feminist ways; they have developed their own voices, vocabulary, and distinctive styles of rhetoric in which irony and shock are prized. For feminists e.g., Gilligan, Manning, Welch, *how* one speaks matters as much as *what* one speaks—a stand that male writers in mainstream ethics (with a few exceptions, Augustine, Milton, and Newman) do not seem to have taken.

All of these features are visible in two recent important works in ethics: Sidney Callahan's *In Good Conscience: Reason and Emotion in Moral Decision Making* (1991), and Rita C. Manning's *Speaking from the Heart: A Feminist Perspective on Ethics* (1992).[17] In the first, Callahan offers an optimistic analysis of the heart's contributions to morality. Her eight untechnical chapters provide a clear picture of a complex phenomenon, one that takes into account new psychological understandings of the self, emotion, reason, intuition, developmental change and problem solving. Central to Callahan's case for realism in making moral decisions is her conviction that complete detachment and objectivity are not only impossible, they are undesirable, since the stronger our convictions and the more we appreciate something, the deeper our affections. Callahan argues that emotion, reason, and intuition should be fully integrated and engaged in our depictions of decision making, that we "need to make decisions in a holistic way that does justice to all our moral resources" (113). She reminds us that "Huck Finn is not the only character in the world who chose correctly following his heart" (139).

Rita Manning recalls that her experiences as a teacher of moral theories taught her the importance of her own moral intuitions: To see that she was misguided about her own commitments in moral philosophy—to the centrality of theory; to the exclusion of all but Kantian and consequentialist accounts; and to a strong version of moral realism (xi–xvi). In place of the ethics one finds in college philosophy and religion texts, Manning argues in favor of a moral theory in which the self is connected rather than isolated; this is a model of reasoning that is contextual rather than abstract, where the normative principles are grounded in experience rather than broad principles grounded in abstract reasoning (28). Manning affirms, as well, an understanding of moral beliefs based upon experience and guidance about practical life, where there are no dichotomies between reason and emotion, mind and body, culture and nature (28). This is an ethics that gives a lot of attention to concrete moral cases, and to stories, poetry, diaries, and journals —literary forms rarely found in traditional ("scientific") ethics. Finally, Manning proposes an ethics that flows from groups rather than individuals, from conversations rather than debates. Her ethics involves "just caring"—for self, children, peers, and animals whether domestic or wild.

In both of these books, as in womanist literature in general, one sees other features of feminist theorists: Support for the democratization of ethics—for opening it up to non-specialists, and for respecting all human experience. Feminists welcome diversity; they encourage interdependence. Ethics, in their view, is distinctive and inclusive—not exclusive. Like jazz musicians, they see growth in active collaboration, strength in mutual support—feminists know that sisterhood builds solidarity. Christians and Marxists, gays and married women have collaborated and influenced each other. In part, these beliefs flow from a postmodern rather than a classic understanding of knowledge and human nature. There is the sense that what an ethicist writes or says possesses the same features as those who create in music, painting, or poetry, and that moral philosophy involves imagination, sensitivity, and creativity. Some of the "unscholastic" and "unscientific" literary devices one finds in feminist studies are the result of widely held beliefs about ethics: That it is a human expression of thought and feeling. Each author is a voice in a choir of voices that collectively approach truth. Feminists, especially those influenced by postmodern philosophers, are at home with the conviction that there is no objective, universally valid knowledge: Human beings are irrevocably individual historical agents, creatures located in time, place, and culture.[18] This compositional rather than analytical model of knowledge, a view that belongs to history more than to chemistry, depicts moral truth as a crystal that is many faceted and multi-dimensional; it considers individual knowledge as always limited by perspective, position, point of view. It accepts the trend currently strong in narrative philosophy that looks not to neo-Kantian reason (autonomous, objective, and universal), but to communities and traditions, to narratives and fundamental metaphors, as the sources of ethical knowledge. In taking this approach, feminist ethics shows its willingness to actively learn from contemporary science; it is forward, not backward, looking.[19]

From the start, feminists working in ethics were critical of some of the controlling assumptions central to the normative principles of mainstream moral theories. For example, both rule-utilitarians and act-utilitarians advocate impartiality: That each person's interests should count equally in moral calculations. Feminists, such as Susan Sherwin, and Marie Giblin, have argued that this demand reflects male thinking; that in reality special concerns and preferences are no less legitimate, and in many cases merited, because of relationships, roles, and respon-sibilities. Feminists were also wary of theories based upon abstract principles, for example Kant's Categorical Imperative, because of their limited usefulness and inadequate guidance. Such principles were thought to be problematic for another reason as well: They lack any affective component, and thereby support distanced objectivity rather than concerned emotionality—contradicting the feminist emphasis on love, deeply felt and abiding, as the basis of enduring hope, joy, and knowledge.[20] Deliberately causing "gender trouble" by showing that life exceeds the bounds imposed by rationality is the special political and philosophical importance of lesbians, according to Judith Butler.[21]

Both the ethics of care, and the ethics of justice have exhibited strong commitments to social action. As Sharon Welch says, "Marxists are right—love for individuals is not enough. Structural change is required" (166). From what has been stated about feminist ethics' problems with mainstream moral theories, it should not surprise us that feminists have abandoned Mill's "Greatest Happiness" principle, and distanced themselves from Hobbes' egoism. Denise Lardner Carmody in her best selling *Virtuous Woman: Reflections on Christian Feminist Ethics* (1992), argues for a number of changes in the Catholic Church's sexual teaching.[22] Further, the paradigms of nurture and friendship embodied in an ethics of "just caring" support concrete action for the liberation of oppressed minorities, and historically disadvantaged groups. "They require action by the oppressed themselves and by those in positions of advocacy for the oppressed," Haney writes (119). The ethics of justice recognizes the importance of rights, autonomy and equality. Both approaches emphasize women's interests and issues of special concern to women, for example, fairer distribution of federal funds for research on mental health, on the impact of pornography, and the links between racism and sexism. "In pursuing feminist ethics, we must continually raise the question, 'What does it mean for women?'" Susan Sherwin states (28).

Honesty and integrity have been major themes in this approach from its beginning. Caring, both as disposition and as expressed in action, is another important theme. Hope and fidelity to being are additional virtues. Annette Baier has employed "appropriate trust" as a concept that effectively bridges an ethics of love and an ethics of duty. Linda A. Bell has advanced an ethics of centering freedom instead of an ethics of care taking, of playfulness instead of control.[23] Starhawk has argued that the basis of ethics is erotic love for the particular, a belief that one finds in Gerard Manley Hopkins's poetry.[24] Marie J. Giblin calls feminist bio-ethics a "prophetic lens" with which we are able to see more clearly the injustices in the health care system and the possibilities for more caring and just communities.[25]

As it approaches the third decade in its modern history, Christian feminists view dimensions of Christ's teaching and life as consistent with and enriching to a feminist ethics, according to Haney (123). Christ's teaching on self-sacrifice, however, is a subject of difficulty for some writers, as is Christ's teaching on the cross, suffering, discipleship, and nonresistance (Farley, 231). "Christianity is prone to an ethics of Christian character, of personal virtue, that is as ahistorical and apolitical in orientation as an unreconstructed ethic of care," Kathryn Tanner observes (188). Emily Culpepper, Sharon Welch, and Mary Daly have been critical of classical monotheism, and have advocated the creation of multiple images and symbols of the Holy. They have emphasized God's immanence rather than God's transcendence; they have seen divinity within relationships and events. Feminist writers, such as Denise Lardner Carmody, have been cautious about Biblical morality because of its patriarchal bias, its violence, and the "dark side of monotheism," to use Regina Schwartz's phrase.[26] Because of the limits seen in the theology and ethics of Paul, Augustine, Aquinas, Luther, and Calvin, Elizabeth Schussler Fiorenza has put forward a widely influential reconstruction of Christian beginnings, while Rosemary Radford Ruether has developed a distinctive feminist theology. Clearly, Christian feminist ethics cannot be called either "theocentric" or "evangelical."

Both Protestant and Roman Catholic feminists have challenged traditional ecclesiology and spirituality because of their patriarchal structures and images that impact negatively upon women's roles and functions within family, society, and church. In recent years, Rosemary Chinnici has invited women to transcend the traditional boundaries and to discover their self-worth through a process of re-imaging the church.[27] Sandra Schneiders has put together themes intended to develop a new concept of religious life for women's religious orders.[28] Leanne McCall Tigert has told the stories of gays, lesbians, and bisexuals in the church in order to offer possibilities for healing changes.[29] Kathleen Fischer has presented a new approach to spiritual direction based upon women's experience and their concern for inclusiveness, connectedness, justice and mutuality.[30]

The Vatican's position on birth control, abortion, and high-tech fertility, its unwillingness to use inclusive language in the text of a recent catechism for use throughout the Roman Catholic Church, as well as its refusal to make any concessions on women's ordination, have angered—but not deterred—Catholic feminists.[31] Finally, Haney considers grace, not as forgiveness but as being at home in the universe—as living gracefully—to be a rich concept (123). Christian feminism has, as we will see, a strong eschatological dimension too (123–24).

A Feminist Ethic for Tomorrow: The Lasting Power of Dangerous Memories

Sharon Welch's *A Feminist Ethic of Risk*, has been called brilliant and provocative, one of the most important books published within the last few years. It is a fine example of current feminist thought. Drawing upon women's literature (Toni Morrison, Paule Marshall, Toni Cade Bambara, Mildred Taylor, Maya Angelou, Adrienne Rich), and women's contributions to science (Sandra Harding), psychology (Carol Gilligan), religion (Carol Christ, Mary Daly, Dorothee Soelle, Emily Culpepper), and ethics (Rosemary Radford Ruether, Susan Griffin, Beverly Wildung Harrison), the book contains an ethical theory that embodies some now familiar feminist methodological themes and emphases, as well as a number of unique and challenging ethical and religious insights.

As we might expect, Welch begins with a critique. She examines middle class ethics in America, in particular the ideology that shapes United States foreign, military, and nuclear policies. Everywhere she finds an "ethics of control" which is characterized by competition, combat, and the avoidance of risk; it is an ethic that places absolute value on power (23–47). For Welch, this ethic is flawed and irrational, full of violence and threat—it cannot be called just, and does not promote world peace. "The predilection for violence has led the United States to intervene repeatedly with military force in Latin America, and it has driven and continues to drive the nuclear arms race," she writes (42). In place of this ethic, Welch proposes an "ethic of risk", one characterized by three elements: The redefinition of responsible action, the grounding in community, and strategic risk taking (20).

Welch's ethic prizes small victories, the gains achieved by women's resistance groups. It values the wisdom she finds in African-American women's writings about the power and hope resident in communities that provide havens of support in struggles and contexts for ongoing struggles (21). Consequently, hers is an ethic of liberation that supports both social change through resistance of evil, and commitment to communal work that brings about lasting, if usually partial, solutions. "The model of maturity central to an ethic of risk leads to a particular type of action, a construction of responsible action as the creation of a matrix of further resistance," she writes (74–75). This means that we measure the appropriateness of a response not simply by its immediate results, but by the possibilities it creates. As well, "Responsible action does not mean one individual resolving the problems of others. It is, rather, participation in a communal work, laying the groundwork for the creative response of people in the present and in the future" (75).

In terms of the process of formulating the decisions that flow from normative principles and guiding rules, Welch's ethic moves away from the individualism and autonomy central to mainstream liberal ethics; she advocates broad communication in decision-making (123), and has none of the atomism found in Fletcher's ethics. Her theory is grounded in the conviction that interaction between multiple communities with divergent principles, norms, and mores is essential for foundational moral critique, and that the moral critique of structural forms of injustice will not emerge within a cohesive community (123–124). Welch's radicalism is seen in her position that we cannot be moral alone (127), since the discernment of norms and strategies requires the active interaction of different communities; to be effective, this interaction requires an openness to others, their history, and experience. "The collective telling of stories is the foundation for seeing and then challenging patterns of systemic injustice," she writes (128). The goal of communicative ethics is not merely passive consensus but mutual critique leading to a more adequate understanding of what is just and how particular forms of justice may be achieved (129).

One goal of Welch's ethics is the building of a "beloved community" (160–161). This community is based on love and respect. From within the matrix of the beloved community there is a solid basis for social critique and self-criticism: The life giving love constitutive of solidarity with the oppressed and love of oneself (161). For Welch, this love is far from a spirit of self-sacrifice (161). With Mary Daly and Audre Lorde, she espouses a love that is joyful, self-restoring, and erotic (170–71). Community means to work with others and not to lose oneself; it means interdependence (161). Community implies responsibility and empowerment. "People are empowered to work for justice by their love for others and by the love they receive from others" (165).

Welch celebrates the immanence of the divine in compassion, joy, learning and erotic love—in the daily graces that lift us to a larger self (174). In her eyes, divinity is a quality made up of relationships, lives, events, and natural processes (177). She is cautious about Protestant theology's emphasis on God's kingship and absolute power (103–122). She finds the god of classical theism irrational and unworthy of worship (175). For Welch, grace is a healing power rather than a saving force (178). Her ethic celebrates a presence that is healing and fragile, constitutive of life and unambiguously present in the human condition (177). Nowhere does one sense that she considers the Bible to be an infallible or absolute authority in ethics, or that the church's moral teaching should be shown special respect. Given her emphasis on active listening to large and diverse communities, on the importance of friendship, love, and care, one concludes that Welch's ethic of risk will use the power of "dangerous memories" to transform not simply society, but the church's institutions and social teachings. It also calls us to work responsibly to emancipate those in today's church who are "the widow, the poor, and the orphan."

Within her critique of liberal ethics and religion, Welch provides a blueprint for bringing about ongoing social change, as well as a set of guiding moral principles. She gives us a summary of a process of moral discernment, and an outline of supportive theological doctrines.

Throughout the presentation of her celebrational ethic, Welch shows her commitment to contemporary feminist thinking in science, politics, literature, ethics, and religion. Her point of view is captured in her final words about recent resistance movements in Africa, Korea, Nicaragua, and the Philippines: "All of these movements are holy; all of them are flawed. Their gains are incomplete: Aims for social justice are hindered by exploitive forces within the movements, and hindered by oppression from without. Middle class people can be empowered by a recognition of the power of divine love and healing at work in our communities of resistance. Our efforts are partial, yet they are divine in their love and courage. They bear witness to the transcendent, healing power of love; they bear witness to the beauty and wonder of life. They are a dangerous memory" (180).

Assessing Feminist Ethics: Weighing Its Worth

Contemporary feminist theory at its best is "the most ethically challenging and intellectually sophisticated exposure of the full dilemmas of our pluralistic and ambiguous postmodern moment," according to David Tracy.[32] Consequently, it is not yet possible at this time to make anything like a final assessment of feminist ethics, its methodology or epistemology, the soundness of its theological or spiritual insights. Some writers, such as Tom Beauchamp and James Childress have pointed out some problems in an ethics of care. It falls short in terms of its completeness, explanatory power, and its ability to justify its conclusions. It is undeveloped, and too contextual and hostile to principles. "Without a broader framework, the ethics of care is too confined to the *private* sphere of intimate relationships and may serve to reinforce an uncritical adherence to traditional social patterns of assigning caretaker roles to women," they write (91). However, while an ethics of care faces some of the same problems inherent in Joseph Fletcher's ethics—care, like love, provides neither explicit rules nor certain guidance when we are faced with complex social or personal issues. It is important to note that recent authors, such as Peta Bowden and Rita Manning have addressed some of the main criticisms, which strengthened this approach. In her review study, "Feminist Ethics after Modernity: Towards an Appropriate Universalism," Susan Parsons argues that liberalism may not furnish the best way for feminist ethics to develop, and other alternatives need to be explored.[33]

Four groups will have special problems with feminist ethics. First, those who see human knowing as inherently objective and universal, naturally transcending the limits of bodies, genders, contexts, and cultures. Such thinkers will be unsympathetic, indeed hostile, toward the feminist understanding of moral decision-making, just as classic Thomists were hostile toward Karl Rahner's theory of personal existentialist knowledge. Secondly, there are those who are not supportive of a morality based on anything less than rationally sound normative principles. George Sher, for instance, is skeptical about Carol Gilligan's claims to have found male bias in existing moral theories.[34] Sher calls "spurious" the suggestion that women's decisions are "concrete" and "contextual" (595). He does not accept Gilligan's observed opposition between personal relationships and impersonal principles. Rational, self-interested Rawlsian contractors always adjust their principles to protect important personal relationships, Sher argues (602). "All things considered, Gilligan's findings seem neither to undermine nor decisively to adjudicate among the familiar options of moral theory. They may edge us in certain theoretical directions, but the movement they compel takes us nowhere near the boundaries of the known territories" (604). In Sher's opinion, "The opposition of concrete and abstract, personal and impersonal, duty and care are not recent empirical discoveries. . . . We have always known that an adequate theory must assign each its proper place" (604).[35]

Thirdly, in spite of the religious features found in Christian feminist theories, this approach will be anathema to Christians who believe that the Bible or the church contains infallible moral teaching that possesses lasting authority over law, science, conscience, and culture. Both conservative Roman Catholics, as well as evangelicals will find feminist ethics apostate, because of its insistence that Scripture and theology can be subject to serious critique and radical change. Finally, there are those who consider feminists naive because they give a special place, indeed a privileged truth-value, to women's moral experiences. Feminist ethics has been influential in nursing largely because of the influence of Nel Noddings's *Caring: A Feminine Approach to Ethics and Moral Education* (1984). It has found little support, however, in the business, trade, military, sports, or political fields where either national or group self-interest dominates. One doubts if feminist thinking will ever come to rule on Wall Street or within the Pentagon; whether an ethics of "just care" will control ownership decisions in major league baseball or professional basketball. Further, the fact that feminists show a preference for the oppressed and minorities—they target institutional injustices—means that they have put themselves in conflict with powerful forces which have nothing to gain either from concession or collaboration. Here lies lasting trouble.[36] On the other hand, feminists' concerns about the obvious inequalities within health care in America and worldwide will find support in some circles. Their prophetic leadership will be welcome, and find a home in communities sensitive about sexism, racism, and educational and economic deprivations. However, they must avoid both the leadership and agenda problems raised by Rene Denfeld in *The New Victorians*, which argues that feminist leaders have become bogged down in extremes, lost touch with reality, and need a new agenda.[37]

Since feminist ethics does not aspire to become a universal moral theory, its humbler and more realistic stance should protect it from competitors with higher ambitions—and probably insure its ability to survive and cross-fertilize. Support for women's studies programs, and for women's health issues, will further protect and strengthen feminist ethics, again provided feminists can separate themselves from those programs that provide nothing more than opportunities for anti-intellectual male bashing, as Daphne Patai and Noreta Koertge argue.[38]

From my own research and teaching experience, I have found that white Anglo-Saxon males and females educated in America's elite universities have problems with Sharon Welch's appeals to the ethical insights within African-American women's literature. Corporate leaders feel frustrated by a decision-making process like Marie Giblin's and Rita C. Manning's that goes beyond experts and includes the "subjugated." To be successful in most management circles, any proposal for change must be practical and efficient, cost-effective and inexpensive— feminist ethics gives little weight to such concerns. In terms of its *Christian* features, feminist ethics scores highly because of its emphasis on "just care" and its concerns for the oppressed. Modern moral theology is being defined, above all, by a "turn to the oppressed," and to the "otherness" in all who are oppressed, Anne E. Patrick rightly notes and this must assist the acceptance of feminist ethics.[39] In spite of its rejection of Western theology's standard images of God, and its reservations about mainstream Christology, feminist ethics is theistic and Christ-centered. Grace and the Spirit have important roles in Welch's theory. Catholic feminists, as we have seen, value liturgical celebrations, the church's sacraments and sacramentals, anointings and blessings in particular. However, traditional Christians find feminist ethics' ecclesiology disturbing, its anticlericalism bitter, and its stress on erotic love embarrassing. The fact that feminist ethics is a liberation ethics (with a Marxist heritage) poses a separate problem.

Conclusion: Feminist Ethics in 2050: A Major Force for Social Change

As future writers describe feminist ethics in the year 2050, I believe that they will see a broad movement that has continued to grow during the century, its influence much wider than in 1997. Such studies will see (I expect) some acceptance worldwide of feminist ethics' calls for broader and more representative decision making, and more support of its efforts to overcome oppression within the church and society. Nurture, caring, hope and joy will be more central virtues within Christian spirituality. Building upon the foundations laid by Mary Daly, Margaret Farley, Lisa Sowle Cahill, Christine Gudorf, Anne E. Patrick, Judith Dwyer, and Elizabeth Johnson, Roman Catholic sexual ethics, the church's social morality, its schools and institutions, its pastoral policies and canon law—in application if not in theory—will bear clearer signs of the saving power of this model of Christian ethics—even if there are still no women bishops in the church.

In liberal and mainstream Protestant communities in Europe, North America, the Pacific, Africa, and Latin America, feminist thought will have reshaped, with differing results, all other models of theology, life and ministry. Rather than a new and minor alternative to mainstream ethical theories, feminist ethics (alongside liberation ethics), will have a major place in biomedical ethics; women's voices will be familiar in law, psychology, sociology, political science, and criminology.

Feminist ethics is celebrating its adolescence today; its future is full of life, health, and promise.

NOTES

[1] Carol Gilligan, *In A Different Voice: Psychological Theory and Women's Development* (Cambridge, MA: Harvard University Press, 1982), 5–23. Also Susan J. Hekman, *Moral Voices, Moral Selves: Carol Gilligan and Feminist Moral Theory* (University Park, PA: Penn State University Press, 1995).

[2] Sharon D. Welch, *A Feminist Ethic of Risk* (Minneapolis, MN: Fortress Press, 1990), 23–47.

[3] Virginia L. Warren, "Feminist Directions in Medical Ethics," in *Feminist Perspectives in Medical Ethics*, edited by Helen Bequaert Holmes and Laura M. Purdy (Bloomington, IN: Indiana University Press, 1992), 32–45.

[4] Eleanor Humes Haney, "What is Feminist Ethics? A Proposal for Continuing Discussion," *Journal of Religious Ethics* 8, 1 (Spring 1980), 115–124.

[5] Margaret A. Farley, "Feminism and Universal Morality," in *Prospects for a Common Morality*, Gene Outka and John P. Reeder, Jr., editors (Princeton, NJ: Princeton University Press, 1993), 170.

[6] On this subject, see Katie G. Cannon, "Response," *Journal of Feminist Studies in Religion* 5, 2 (1989), 92ff.

[7] For a valuable survey of recent developments in Christian feminist ethics, Kathryn Tanner, "The Care that Does Justice: Recent Writings in Feminist Ethics and Theology," *Journal of Religious Ethics* 24, 1 (Spring 1996), 171–191.

[8] For an overview of feminist themes, *What is Feminism?*, Juliet Mitchell and Ann Oakley, editors (New York, NY: Pantheon Books, 1986).

[9] Susan Sherwin, "Feminist and Medical Ethics: Two Different Approaches to Contextual Ethics," in *Feminist Perspectives in Medical Ethics*, (Toronto: Canadian Scholar's Press, Inc., 1993), 17–31.

[10] Rosemarie Tong, *Feminine and Feminist Ethics* (Belmont, CA: Wadsworth Publishing, 1993), 5.

[11] On this subject, Elizabeth A. Johnson, *Woman, Earth and Creator Spirit* (Mahwah, NJ: Paulist Press, 1993); Sallie McFague, *The Body of God: An Ecological Theology* (Minneapolis, MN: Fortress Press, 1993).

[12] On central aspects of this approach in bioethics, cf. Special Issue: "Feminist Perspectives on Bioethics," *Kennedy Institute of Ethics Journal* 6, 1 (March 1996).

[13] On these subjects, Joan M. Merdinger, "Women, Death, and Dying," and Juliette S. Silva, "Mexican-American Women: Death and Dying," in *A Cross-Cultural Look at Death, Dying, and Religion,* Joan K. Parry and Angela Shen Ryan, editors (Chicago, IL: Nelson-Hall Publishers, 1995).

[14] On this subject, Susan Muller Okin. *Justice, Gender and the Family* (New York, NY: Basic Books, 1989), 23.

[15] Annette Baier, "Trust and Antitrust," *Ethics* 96 (1986), 231–260.

[16] Margaret A. Farley, "Feminist Ethics," in *The Westminster Dictionary of Christian Ethics*, edited by James Childress and John Macquarrie (London: Westminster Press, 1986), 229–231, at 230.

[17] Rita C. Manning, *Speaking from the Heart: A Feminist Perspective on Ethics* (Lanham, MD: Rowman & Littlefield, 1992).

[18] On this subject, Georgia Masters Keightley, "The Challenge of Feminist Theology," *Horizons*, 14 (1987), 262–282; Carol P. Christ, "Embodied Thinking: Reflections on Feminist Theological Method," *Journal of Feminist Studies in Religion* 5 (1989).

[19] This is obvious from the essays in such works as *Feminist Ethics and Social Theory: A Sourcebook*, edited by Diana Tietjens Meyers (Florence, KY: Routledge, 1997).

[20] For a review of this subject, as well as an important critique, William C. Spohn, "Passions and Principles," in *Notes in Moral Theology*, 1990, *Theological Studies* 52, 1 (1991), 69–87.

[21] Judith Butler, *Gender Trouble: Feminism and the Subversion of Identity* (London: Routledge, 1990).

[22] Also on this subject, *Redefining Sexual Ethics,* Susan E. Davies, and Eleanor Humes Haney, editors (Cleveland, OH: Pilgrim Press, 1991).

[23] Linda A. Bell, *Rethinking Ethics in the Midst of Violence: A Feminist Approach to Freedom* (Lanham, MD: Rowman & Littlefield, 1993).

[24] Starhawk, *Dreaming the Dark: Magic, Sex and Politics* (Boston, MA: Beacon Press, 1982), 44.

[25] Marie J. Giblin, "The Prophetic Role of Feminist Bioethics," *Horizons*, 24, 1 (1997), 37–49.

[26] Regina Schwartz, *The Curse of Cain: The Violent Legacy of Monotheism* (Chicago, IL: University of Chicago Press, 1997).

[27] Rosemary Chinnici, *Can Women Re-Image the Church?* (Mahwah, NJ: Paulist Press, 1992).

[28] Sandra M. Schneiders, *Re-imagining Religious Life Today* (Mahwah, NJ: Paulist Press, 1993).

[29] Leanne McCall Tigert, *Coming Out While Staying In* (Cleveland, OH: United Church Press, 1994).

[30] Kathleen Fischer, *Women at the Well: Feminist Perspectives on Spiritual Direction* (Mahwah, NJ: Paulist Press, 1993).

[31] On this subject, Christine E. Gudorf, "Encountering the Other: The Modern Papacy on Women," in *Social Compass* (Louvain) 36, 3 (1989), 295–310.

[32] For Tracy's views of this approach, David Tracy, *Plurality and Ambiguity Hermeneutics, Religion, Hope* (San Francisco: Harper and Row, 1987), 69, 71, 76–77, 80, 100, 109, 112, 131, 133, 135–136, 139.

[33] Susan Parsons, "Feminist Ethics after Modernity: Towards an Appropriate Universalism," *Studies in Christian Ethics* 8, 1 (1995), 77–94.

[34] George Sher, "Other Voices, Other Rooms? Women's Psychology and Moral Theory," in *Moral Philosophy: Selected Readings*, 2nd edition (Orlando, FL: Harcourt Brace College Publishers, 1996), 593–604.

[35] For other points of criticism, see Rosemary Tong, *Feminine and Feminist Ethics*, Ibid., 80–107.

[36] For a summary and critique of Noddings's ethics, Rosemarie Tong, *Ibid.*, 108–134.

[37] Rene Denfeld, *The New Victorians* (New York, NY: Warner Books, 1995).

[38] Daphne Patai and Noreta Koertge, *Professing Feminism* (New York, NY: Basic Books, 1994).

[39] Anne E. Patrick, "The Linguistic Turn and Moral Theology," *Catholic Theological Society of America Proceedings*, 42 (1987), 51.

CHAPTER 2

Evangelical Ethics

Millions of Christians are committed to the belief that "Christian morality" means the faith-filled, life, and behavior responses to the God who has given a unique and final revelation to guide women and men in their efforts to live as God's people: The Bible. For many Presbyterians, Southern Baptists, Seventh-Day Adventists, Missouri and Wisconsin Synod Lutherans, the Bible—God's Word—is both the groundwork and final court of appeal in religious ethics. Assuredly, reason and science, Aristotle and Augustine are helpful guides for Christians as they strive to live righteously in the modern world, but the Almighty's guidance found in the Bible—lasting, inerrant—provides God's rules of faith and practice.

Sharing some of the same assumptions as found in natural law ethics, situation ethics, and liberation ethics, this approach has its own distinctive moral method, goals, and religious supports. It is a deontological model of Christian ethics that has deep roots and powerful appeal.

The Bible: The Rule of Faith and Life

Understanding moral experience is one of the aims of ethics. However, as Thomas W. Ogletree observes, ethics, whether religious or philosophical, can never be simply descriptive: It must undertake normative proposals of human ways of being and acting in the world. It must offer guidance about the morality of capital punishment, political misinformation, and homosexual marriage.[1] Some Christian feminists derive their proposals from women's experience; they resolve issues on the basis of the truth and goodness that women find in nurture and caring. Those who espouse natural law theories develop what they consider to be coherent visions of the moral life from their analyses of the "face of nature": The teleological patterns and potentialities believed to provide insight into God's will for humanity.

Those Christian ethicists who turn to the Bible rather than to women's experiences or, to nature's face in order to formulate normative moral principles, take this turn primarily because they hold a set of crucial beliefs about the Bible. First, that the canonical Scriptures are the Word

Conservative
evangelical
Not all

of God. Second, that they are the sole infallible and inerrant rule of faith and life, and third, that these writings are the highest authority for doctrine and morals.

Associated with broad movements committed to the proclamation and defense of biblical Christianity, this conservative or evangelical view of Scripture argues that God is the Bible's ultimate source; that God cannot lie or contradict himself; therefore the Bible cannot contain errors or inconsistencies. More positively, the conviction that God is the source of Scripture means (for a large number of Christians in North America, Europe, Asia, Latin America, and the Pacific) that the Bible is a unique body of truth that is free from factual error in its statements about history, geography, philosophy, as well as religion and ethics, because as Paul J. Achtemeier says, "God preserved the authors of Scripture from error in these matters as well as in matters more properly pertaining to its central message of human salvation."[2]

These Christians, whose number has grown worldwide during the 1980s–1990s, are motivated by a desire to take the Bible seriously; they see it as their role to place human experience under the Bible's judgments. Consequently, they believe that they have a responsibility as Christians to make sure that state and federal laws about abortion, school prayer, marriage, divorce, business, health, welfare, and the penal system are "biblical."

For Clark H. Pinnock, an American Baptist evangelical Christian, the Bible embodies God's Revelation; it is a product of Revelation, and a component of God's revealing activity.[3] Pinnock sees his belief that the Bible is the unique locus of God's word, the "canon and yardstick of Christian truth," to be firmly based in two important sources: First, it is part of an almost universal Christian consensus that goes back to at least the second century (a belief we find, for instance, in Augustine's letter 82 to Jerome). Second, it is present within the Bible itself in its own statements about Revelation in creation (Psalm 19:1), about an "infinite, personal God making himself known as the saving Lord who desires a covenant relationship with his human creatures" (8). As well, there are the Bible's teachings about Christ (10–11), and the coming of the Spirit at Pentecost (12).

Further signs of this belief about the Bible are seen in such places as Exodus 19:5: "Now therefore, if you will obey my voice and keep my covenant, you shall be my own possession among all the peoples." In Jeremiah 7:21, 23, we find: "Thus says the Lord of hosts, the God of Israel: . . . 'Obey my voice, and I will be your God, and you shall be my people; and walk in all the ways that I command you, that it may be well with you.'" There is II Timothy 3:16, which says that all Scripture is inspired by God; and there is II Peter 1:20–21, which affirms that prophets moved by the Holy Spirit, spoke from God. Shadows of this attitude can be seen as well in the Gospels, Mark 7:8; 10:19; Luke 18:20; and John 17:17.

Evangelical ethicists maintain that the Bible is not simply a witness to revelation: It is revelation. The Scriptures are revelation in writing. Pinnock reflects this view when he says, "Inspired Scripture constitutes a term in the rich pattern of revelation given to humanity in Jesus Christ. It is a capstone and completion of it in the sense that it conveys in a reliable manner the freight and burden of revelation secured in an appropriate form by God's own action" (16). The Bible, according to Pinnock, is the primary witness to Christ, an important part of revelation but not the whole, one of the forms of God's revelation through which the light reaches us—a "durable and objective record of the burden of divine revelation, engendered by the Spirit, and given to bring us to the saving knowledge of God" (16).

Further, because the Bible's inspiration (understood as inerrancy) guarantees an error-free Bible, one can have certainty—the soundest basis—about Scripture's truth and trustworthiness. Here lies the basis for the evangelical Christian's conviction that authentic truth lies in the Bible's moral experience, its ethical vision, and normative principles.

These Christians hold several other beliefs about the Bible that are important in terms of their ethics. Rather than seeing the Bible as a collection of books or narratives of limited religious or moral value for contemporary Christians because they were written in foreign languages millennia ago, Evangelicals maintain that since all parts of the Bible are equally inspired, then all parts of the Bible are equally revelational. Also, they insist that not only the thoughts conveyed by the Bible's words, but also God, through the Holy Spirit, has inspired the very words themselves.

Thus, the major task of these Biblical scholars becomes clear: To demonstrate the inspirational and revelational quality of Scripture by showing that the Bible has an enduring "macropurpose," and what God wants to teach through Scripture remains an error-free unity. One finds signs of these methodological principles in Pinnock's thought: Christians must return to the biblical pattern of revelation because: "Revelation, according to the Bible and historic theology, is not merely subjective and existentialist, but a meaningful disclosure of the gracious God who acts and speaks. It supplies us with the crucial information about the character and purposes of God, given in creaturely modalities we can understand, that enables people to be reconciled with God. It enables us to become acquainted with God so that we might meet him and know him" (27).

Other evangelicals hold similar views. For Ronald S. Toth, writing in *The Plain Truth* (1986), there is not one single facet of life upon which the Bible does not touch and, in principle, tell people what to do. It is the inspired, revealed, and unchanging teaching for our lives. For Carl H. Mischke, president of the Wisconsin Evangelical Lutheran Synod (which had 418,000 members in 1987), the Bible is infallible. Therefore, women cannot be ordained as priests or pastors, because of what one finds in Ephesians 5:21; I Timothy 2:11–15; I Corinthians 11:3, 14:33–36.[4] For Norman L. Shoaf, also writing in *The Plain Truth* (November–December 1987), "Dozens of Bible examples show how people who obeyed God's laws about honesty, along with other revealed laws and statutes, succeeded in spite of giant odds against them" (15). We are able to follow God's law; it always succeeds—"It is the only intelligent course to follow"(15). While Pinnock takes a somewhat less conservative line (the Bible does not teach a doctrine of complete inerrancy, in his opinion), nevertheless, the Bible is trustworthy in the fundamental sense. He writes, "In telling us what God has said and done, it [the Bible] brings us to a saving knowledge of him and builds us up in our holy faith" (75–76). The Bible contains God's propositional truths that we should seek to shape our moral lives.

Evangelicals hold a definite position about the relationship between the Bible, church, and culture. Scripture needs the church as its bulwark (80). However, the Bible stands above tradition, and outside the Church—it is God's Word. "The church can fall into error and needs the Bible to measure herself by. In turn, the church serves the canon by continuing in the truth and faithfully proclaiming the Word of God" (82). For Christians like Pinnock, the Bible also stands over culture and is the supreme critic of the thoughts and intents of the human heart (95)—a position quite different from liberal Protestants, feminists, and the majority of American Catholics.

For liberal Protestants, the sum total of human experience, secular and sacred, is the highest authority in ethics, science, or history. For feminists, women's experience provides a corrective to the Bible's patriarchal morality. For Roman Catholics, the church and tradition limit Scripture's epistemic authority. *The Catechism of the Catholic Church* says that Sacred Scripture is "the speech of God as it is put down in writing under the breath of the Holy Spirit" (81); that Tradition "transmits in its entirety the Word of God which has been entrusted to the apostles by Christ the Lord and the Holy Spirit" (81). Therefore, "as a result the Church, to whom the transmission and interpretation of Revelation is entrusted, does not derive her certainty about all revealed truths from Scripture alone. Both Scripture and Tradition must be accepted and honored with equal sentiments of devotion and reverence" (82).

Pinnock recognizes that today's culture is quite different from that of the Near East in the days of Moses; in interpreting the Bible he has to take the gaps between these two worlds into account. Nevertheless, he is convinced that the Bible's message about the living God who sent the Son to be the world's Savior is not incommunicable today or lacking in any moral or doctrinal authority. "Exactly in the way in which that same message challenged the polytheism and magic of the ancient world, it [the Bible] can today undercut the presuppositions of atheism and pantheism that underlie these objections to biblical authority," Pinnock writes (95).

Before we look at one example of this approach, a final remark is necessary. It can be argued that each model of Christian ethics, even the most rational or philosophical, is "biblical," because Christian ethicists, whether Episcopalian or Roman Catholic, Presbyterian, Lutheran or Greek Orthodox, all share similar beliefs about the Bible. In a sense this is true. Earl H. Brill's *The Christian Moral Vision,* a book prepared for use within the Episcopal Church, states that "Christians naturally turn to the Bible for moral guidance, for the Bible is our fundamental authority in religious matters."[5] One can make the case as well that Joseph Fletcher's situation ethics is "biblical" on the grounds that Scripture is its primary literary source for ethical norms. Also, the recently published *Catechism of the Catholic Church* says: that "the Church has always venerated the Scriptures as she venerates the Lord's Body" (103); that the Church constantly finds her nourishment and strength in sacred Scripture, for the Church welcomes Scripture "not as a human word, 'but as what it really is, the word of God'" (104); and in these sacred books, "the Father who is in heaven comes lovingly to meet his children and talks to them" (104).

However, while there are individual differences among evangelical ethicists (just as one finds in any group of Freudian psychologists, or jazz musicians), those we associate with this approach are united in the conviction that the Bible is God's "very" Word, infallible and inerrant for Christian faith and life. And they stand together in the conviction that their belief about the Bible should control the Christian moralists' goals and methods in the task of formulating normative principles in business, environmental, sexual or biomedical ethics. One such Christian ethicist is John Jefferson Davis.

Evangelical Ethics: Discerning God's Revealed Will in Concrete Situations

Davis's *Evangelical Ethics: Issues Facing the Church Today* (1985) is an up to date and informative examination of such subjects as contraception, homosexuality, euthanasia, capital punishment, civil disobedience, and the morality of war in a nuclear age.[6] Addressed to the Christian pastor and layperson, the opening chapter provides a summary of the author's aims and moral method. Unlike Joseph Fletcher, Davis begins with a defense of obedience to God's commandments. "Though obedience to the law of God can never be the basis for earning one's salvation, nevertheless the clear teaching of the apostle Paul is that the law in and of itself is holy, just, and good (Romans 7:12). Genuine Christian love motivates the believer to fulfill the requirements of the law (cf. Romans 13:10)," Davis writes (8).

Further, supporting Calvin's teaching, Davis sees the law as the "instrument" for learning more thoroughly the nature of God's will and becoming confirmed in the understanding of it (9). Immediately we see Davis's commitment to "Word of God" ethics. Using insights into Jesus' ethics found in Rudolf Schnackenburg's writings, and W.D. Davies's New Testament research, Davis proposes a prescriptive and deontological approach in which "The teachings of Scripture are the final court of appeal for ethics. Human reason, church, tradition, and the natural and social sciences may aid moral reflection, but divine revelation, found in the canonical Scriptures of the Old and New Testaments, constitutes the 'bottom line' of the decision making process" (9).

In Davis's view, as we strive to discern God's will in concrete situations, the Bible functions normatively through its specific commands and precepts, general principles, various precedents, and overall world view (9). This means that some commands can be directly translated into present contexts like the "Do not commit adultery;" some general biblical principles have crucial implications for modern ethical issues such as sacredness of life made in God's image (Genesis 1:26, 28). Practices such as tithing can function as precedents that assist us as we seek to fulfill our stewardship obligations, to understand our specific duties (9–10).

From the start, Davis resists Fletcher's separation of law from love. He argues that "The love of God shed abroad in the heart of the believer is indeed the dynamic motivation of Christian behavior, but this love demonstrates itself in harmony with, and not apart from, the specific commands and precepts of Holy Scripture" (10). This means that authentic love for God is demonstrated by keeping his commandments (John 14:21).

Reason has an essential place in ethics, according to Davis. His evangelical ethics does not disdain logic, nor dismiss the role of the human intellect. However, reason does not act independently of Scripture in his ethics. And since the intellect is impaired by sin, it does not serve as a separate norm standing over against Scripture. Rather, reason is the servant of divine revelation in the application and extension of biblical truth (11). This means that the Christian ethicist will seek all the relevant facts, and weigh them carefully—something one finds throughout Davis's book—but that he or she will interpret them with a mind renewed by the Holy Spirit, and within a framework of meaning controlled by the teachings of Holy Scripture (11–12). In other words, the Christian ethicist seeks all useful information from the social sciences in his or her analysis of homosexuality, for instance, but will use the Bible as the controlling source of moral truth about this behavior (11).

For Davis, there are many moral absolutes, not just one as Fletcher has argued. How do we resolve conflicts between these principles and their resulting duties? Do we use Fletcher's solution? Do we follow the advice of W.D. Ross, or do we employ "proportionalism"? Davis proposes what he calls "contextual absolutism" (14). In each and every ethical situation, no matter how extreme, there is one course that is morally right and free of sin, he believes (14). This is the right way—the way of escape that God has promised. In some cases, this road will require suffering or even martyrdom—the cost of discipleship in some cases—the way of Jesus, the believer's moral ideal in the New Testament, and the way of Daniel and his friends who were willing to suffer and die rather than compromise their convictions by committing an act of idolatry (Daniel 3:17,18). Contextual absolutism cannot support Mrs. Bergmeir's "loving" solution to her dilemma, as Joseph Fletcher advocates.

Finally, Davis's opening chapter takes up some of the problems facing Christians who desire to have their ethics reflected in American law and public policy. His conclusions are sensitive and prudent. Since believers live in a pluralistic society which does not recognize the authority of Scripture, Christians seeking to influence law and public policy must be sensitive not only to basic biblical and theological principles, but to practical considerations as well (19). At times, a prophetic minority may be called to create a consensus on a given issue such as the abolitionists in the last century. At other times, legal change may come first and community consensus later as seen in the 1960s civil rights movement. Churches should be careful, given their limited time and energy, to focus on issues that have special urgency for the body politic; they need to realize both the value and limitation of civil law as an instrument of social change (20). "Civil laws that are consistent with the teachings of Scripture point society to a higher standard of righteousness, which is fulfilled only in Jesus Christ," Davis concludes. "Such laws remain a worthy object of Christian concern and social action" (20).

Davis consistently applies his ethical method in his analysis of contraception (21–61). After looking at the methods of birth control, the Roman Catholic and Protestant, and in particular the evangelical Protestant, positions, he concludes: "It may be argued, then, that contraception can be justified in terms of the general teachings of Scripture concerning the nature of man and Christian marriage. It does not follow, however, that the use of contraception would be right in all circumstances" (50). Davis uses his approach in reaching conclusions about premarital sex (52–55), sex education in public schools (55–56), and world population growth (57–61). "American evangelicals are quite aware—at least in principle—of the biblical mandate for the Great Commission (Matthew 28:19, 20)," he writes. "They need to rediscover the relevance of the Cultural Mandate to 'be fruitful and multiply' (Genesis 1:28). God wants his kingdom to expand through evangelism and through the raising up of a godly seed (Malachi 2:15)" (61).

The author's chapters on the morality of homosexuality (106–128), abortion (129–157), infanticide and euthanasia (158–192), provide further signs of Davis's evangelical ethical method at work. His chapter on homosexuality contains precise information on the history, anthropology, and medical aspects of this subject. Then it looks at the Scriptural witness, and concludes: "Both the Old and New Testament are unequivocal in their teaching that homosexuality is contrary to the moral law, and only the most forced and arbitrary modes of biblical interpretation can conclude otherwise" (122). In the face of serious pastoral concerns, and the pressure of the argument that biblical revelation is distorted by Jewish culture, Davis stands fast: "The church cannot compromise the fundamental biblical teaching: Homosexuality is contrary to the divine will for human sexuality" (124). On the subject of abortion, he is equally definite: "The biblical ethic upholds the dignity and worth of every human being, regardless of the state of development or physical dependency, from the moment of conception until natural death" (157). Finally, after providing a summary of the historical, legal, medical, and psychological aspects of infanticide, Davis again uses Scripture to argue: that the basic thrust of medicine should always be to choose life (cf. Deuteronomy 30:19), because all human life is sacred to God who made it (174). Secondly, that from the perspective of the Judeo-Christian tradition, euthanasia violates the commandment 'You shall not murder' (Exodus 20:13). His conclusion: "The taking of human life—for whatever motives—is strictly forbidden in Scripture, except in those very narrowly defined circumstances such as justifiable war, self-defense, and capital punishment" (191).

Throughout *Evangelical Ethics*, Davis shows that he is aware of current debates in religious and philosophical ethics. He cites the opinions of writers whose insights are central to this book: Joseph Fletcher, Richard McCormick, John Rawls, Paul Ramsey, James Luther Adams, James Childress, John Howard Yoder, James Gustafson, Mary Kenny, David Hollenbach, Ann Fadiman, and Pope John Paul II. His sources are both Catholic and Protestant; they are English, Canadian, German, Italian, and American. However, Davis is faithful to the evangelical principles we have seen in Pinnock, and developed by Carl F.H. Henry, and Cornelius Van Til.[7] For Davis, Christian ethics is concerned not with personal preferences or human feelings; it does not seek to be politically correct. Rather it embodies an uncompromising defense of the fundamental Christian truth: Scripture, God's Word, is the infallible and inerrant rule for life and faith, and the Christian's, indeed, the world's highest authority in ethics. Christians should live by and actively promote Scriptural morality within their communities.

Word of God Ethics: Critical Concerns

As indicated already, both Catholic and Protestant ethicists consider the Bible to be authoritative. However, the majority does not see the Bible's authority in ethics as evangelicals do, nor do they use Scripture to resolve moral issues in the same way that Davis and other Christian conservatives do. For example, Edouard Hamel, Dean of the Faculty of Theology at the Gregorian University in Rome during the 1970s, sounds like Pinnock and Davis in some of his reflections on the place of Scripture in moral theology: "Scripture is a rendezvous with God who in it, through it and in each part of it speaks to people of all ages," Hamel writes.[8] Further, because "biblical morality is guaranteed by Revelation, it will be the faithful and abiding mirror of human morality and it will, if necessary, correct the indications that come from reason" (110). In Hamel's eyes, following Vatican II, the Bible contains "a permanent message of salvation" (113); it provides us with "a sure light" that illuminates complex human problems (110). We are able to find in Scripture "a fundamental sexual anthropology that will tell us, if the hermeneutic effort is properly carried out, what God thinks of human sexuality"(113). As well, the Bible provides us with "an integral vision that will enable us to find more concrete answers with greater certainty" (113); and, in this sense, "it is fair to say that there is no moral problem on which the Bible is totally silent" (113). Finally, when Christians address concrete problems, they (like Paul) should apply a morality that is based on convictions that are theological, eschatological, and Christological, Hamel argues (129–130).

However, for Hamel, the Bible is not the sole source of morality for Christians (115). Scripture must be interpreted by the church using a method that updates the Bible's text in a way that reveals God's saving will (115). The paths of revelation and reason come together, in Hamel's judgment, since God wants what is good for humankind, and what God wants is also what is good for humankind (115). For Hamel, the divine will known by revelation is simply one of the elements—but not the only one—that enables us to know in what our true good consists (115).

The American Roman Catholic ethicist Charles Curran also presents a number of reasons in support of the position that the Bible should have a limited role in Christian ethics.[9] "The biblical renewal has emphasized the historical and cultural limitations of the Scriptures so that one cannot just apply the Scriptures in a somewhat timeless manner to problems existing in different historical circumstances," Curran writes (187). The Scriptures do not confront many of the moral problems we face today (187); they teach little or no social morality (187). What they teach is often colored by eschatological considerations which make it difficult to apply them directly to any contemporary situation (187). Curran sees vast differences between the biblical and the contemporary contexts (187); he finds major problems in any effort to provide a synthesis or systematic understanding of biblical morality (190). For these reasons, Curran cannot accept either an ethical method which considers Christian ethics to be distinctive from other ethics, or an ethics in which the Bible is normative in itself (198). Christians must reflect on the moral experience found in Scripture, Curran admits, but they must also reflect on the experience of others as well, because, in his view, the ethical wisdom and knowledge in the Bible is quite similar to—not different from—the moral experience of all humankind (206).

Two writers who have written in detail about the Bible's authority in Christian ethics are James Gustafson and Gerard J. Hughes. Both argue that the Bible should play a limited role in ethics; both give the Bible no infallible weight in Christian moral decision-making. In a highly respected study that takes the 1970 United States invasion of Cambodia as its test-case, Gustafson, whose theocentric ethics we will examine shortly, sets his own understanding of the use and authority of Scripture within the context of the views of colleagues' writings in Christian ethics.[10] In his view, the Bible does not have the authority of verbal inspiration, as evangelicals claim (175). Nor does the Bible contain the revelation of "a morality" that is authoritative for the judgments of Christians (as Davis holds). Further, Gustafson does not see one controlling "method of ethics" in the Bible, but several different methods that the modern ethicist will choose from on the basis of his or her theological and philosophical principles (175–76). Finally, he does not consider Scripture alone to be the final court of appeal for Christian ethics (176). However, for Gustafson, the Bible does contain a revelation of "theological principles" that can be used to interpret what God is doing in the world (160); these principles provide "clues" to what we, as moral agents, ought to do in particular circumstances (160).

In looking at the different ways that contemporary Christian ethicists use Scripture, Gustafson separates himself from four groups. First, he does not support the idea of the Bible as a source of moral laws (160–161). Second, he does not agree with the notion that the Bible is filled with moral ideals (161–162). Third, he does not like the position of those who hold that "those actions of persons and groups are to be judged morally wrong which are similar to actions that are judged to be wrong or against God's will under similar circumstances in Scripture or are discordant with actions judged to be right or in accord with God's will in Scripture" (163). Fourth, because of its "looseness," he sees major problems in the position of those who maintain that the Bible is simply one of the informing sources for moral judgments, but it is not sufficient in itself to make any particular judgment authoritative (165).

On the positive side, in his efforts to make a Christian moral judgment about the United States invasion of Cambodia, Gustafson rules out using the Bible to provide "proof-texts" as not defensible (168). "To cite the command 'Thou shalt not kill' is not sufficient to defend the judgment that the invasion of Cambodia is morally wrong," he states (168). He also rejects applying biblical morality from an ancient time in a casuistic way (172), because, although the American invasion of Cambodia is not unlike many previous invasions in history, it is not the same as any previous invasion in its character (172).

However, Gustafson does consider the Bible to be a powerful guiding light within society and the church for a variety of reasons: Scripture is an important informing moral source within Western culture (168–69); and the Bible provides data and concepts for understanding the human situation, both in terms of its limits and possibilities (169). Furthermore, the Bible contains "an account of the sorts of human actions and events which morally and religiously serious communities of the past have seen to be in accord and out of accord with the purposes of God for man" (170).

This is Gustafson's preferred understanding of the role of Scripture in ethics: It is a central source for the Christian community in its efforts to discern what God is enabling and requiring men and women to be and to do in particular natural, historical, and social circumstances (176). However, Gustafson does not look upon the Bible as the sole source for Christian discernment. "In judging the Cambodian invasion to be morally wrong one is informed by and appeals to many other bases than scripture," he states (171). Scripture alone is clearly insufficient as a ground for assessing the consequences of human actions, in his estimate (174). The Bible provides orientation toward particular judgments, and informs moral judgments—but it does not by itself determine what they ought to be (176). As Gustafson writes: "Ultimately for Christian ethics, a biblically informed theology provides the bases for the final test of the validity of particular judgments. Christian judgments ought to be consistent, consonant, and coherent with the themes that are generalized to be most pervasive or primary to the biblical witness. But this is not to suggest that the judgments are solely derived from the scriptures . . . (171)."

The Jesuit scholar, Gerard Hughes, provides three specific arguments in support of his position that any attempt to appeal to the Bible as the ultimate authority in ethics runs into major problems.[11] First, Hughes claims that while we must respect Scripture as inspired by God, we must also recognize that the Bible is a collection of thoroughly human documents that were written at particular times and places with specific audiences in mind. This means that we cannot be completely sure that we have understood the Bible's moral teaching, because of the exegetical (language and textual) difficulties we face. For instance, the correct meaning of *porneia* in Matthew's words about divorce (12). In Hughes' view, "we are simply at too great a remove from the texts to be entirely confident that we have understood them correctly" (13). Second, we face serious problems in our efforts to translate the Bible's moral teaching into our cultures, and to apply it to contemporary business and health care issues (14–16). We have these problems largely because the Bible does not provide us with any method of deciding which circumstances are morally significant (16).

Third, while Hughes supports the Second Vatican Council's position that the Bible is inspired, and inerrant concerning "that truth which God wanted put into the sacred writings for the sake of our salvation," he is not convinced that specific moral teachings such as Paul's pastoral teaching on the marriage of virgins, or on meats offered to idols, have the status of "salvation-truths" (18). Such teaching is pastoral advice ("individual moral assertion") and nothing more, according to Hughes (18). It should not be given the weight of truth that leads to salvation. He writes: "In short, I would welcome attempts to spell out in detail the traditional position that revelation is concerned with the details of morality, and not just with the general importance of being morally good. Unless this is done satisfactorily, the question of using revelation as the ultimate authority in ethics simply does not arise at all" (18–19). Thus, he puts in doubt the authority of most of the Bible's moral teaching.[12]

Evangelical Ethics: Constantly Challenging Christians

On May 12, 1879, Pope Leo XIII gave a cardinal's hat to John Henry Newman, arguably the most important English-speaking theologian in the last two hundred years, and one of the major influences on the Second Vatican Council. In his acceptance speech, Newman summed up his life's work as an effort to combat liberalism in theology. His words, filled with emotion, recall how, at an early age in his intellectual development, he had come to see the implications for religion in the writings of those who put reason above Scripture, tradition, and church. Newman described how, first as an Anglican, then later as a Roman Catholic, he had written and preached, counseled students, attempted to establish a university in Ireland, and founded high schools and oratories—out of love and concern for truth.

In its own way, evangelical ethics is a radical approach to combating liberalism and "man-centered autonomy" in contemporary societies.[13] It calls Christians back to their conservative roots. It is counter-cultural, although seemingly unscientific and consciously anti-liberal. However, evangelical ethics, as we have seen, is based upon classic Christian beliefs, and it has a long history. Further, it is clear, consistent, coherent, appealing in its simplicity both in its moral method and its application to current issues. As well, it is a model of Christian ethics that constantly challenges us because of its unwavering faith in the Bible, and its uncompromising efforts to promote Scriptural morality within communities. As the 21st century begins, evangelical ethics will continue to grow in influence and to attract support among conservative Christians worldwide.

NOTES

[1] Thomas W. Ogletree, *The Use of the Bible in Christian Ethics* (Philadelphia: Fortress Press, 1983), 1.

[2] Paul J. Achtemeier, *The Inspiration of Scripture: Problems and Proposals* (Philadelphia: Westminster Press, 1980), 51.

[3] Clark H. Pinnock, *The Scripture Principle* (San Francisco: Harper & Row: 1984), ix.

[4] Kevin Warneke, "Wisconsin Synod Chief Says Bible is Infallible" (*Omaha World-Herald*, Saturday, October 24, 1987), 15.

[5] Earl H. Brill, *The Christian Moral Vision* (New York: Seabury Press, 1979), 47.

[6] John Jefferson Davis, *Evangelical Ethics: Issues Facing the Church Today* (Phillipsburg, NJ: Presbyterian and Reformed Publishing Company, 1985).

[7] On the role of F.H. Henry and Cornelius Van Til in evangelical theology, Harvie M. Conn, *Contemporary World Theology: A Layman's Guide* (Phillipsburg, NJ: Presbyterian and Reformed Publishing Company, 1973).

[8] Edouard Hamel, "Scripture: The Soul of Moral Theology?" in *The Use of Scripture in Moral Theology*, in *Readings in Moral Theology #4*, edited by Charles E. Curran and Richard A. McCormick (New York: Paulist Press, 1984), 105–132, at 130.

[9] Charles Curran, "The Role and Function of the Scriptures in Moral Theology," *Ibid.*, 178–212.

[10] James M. Gustafson, "The Place of Scripture in Christian Ethics: A Methodological Study," *Ibid.*, 151–177.

[11] Gerard J. Hughes, *Authority in Morals: An Essay in Christian Ethics* (Georgetown: Georgetown University Press, 1978).

[12] For Hughes, "The ultimate authority in ethics is to be found in the facts about ourselves and our world on which morality rests, as these are organized in an acceptable ethical theory" (95).

[13] On the rise of evangelical theology and ethics, Harvie M. Conn, op. cit., 4–25.

CHAPTER 3

Natural Law Ethics

C hristian moralists have wrestled for centuries with the relationship between religious ethics and moral philosophy. John Stuart Mill thought that his ethical "model" caught the essence of Christianity; Mill was convinced that his ethic of "utility" embodied Jesus' golden rule. Immanuel Kant, as he developed his duty-based "model," was confident that his "Categorical Imperative" provided a solid basis for resolving moral dilemmas. With its gaze fixed on the "Book of Nature" rather than the "Book of Scripture," and confident that morality is more securely grounded when it rests on reason's objective and inherently empirical conclusions rather than on God's Will (as James Gustafson believes), or Jesus' "revealed" teaching that must be accepted on religious faith (because essentially beyond reason's limits), the "natural law" tradition has a long history in Protestant and Roman Catholic ethics.

Christians, from the start, were attracted to Cicero's stoicism with its emphasis on courage, calmness, and the governing power of natural law. During the 13th century, Aquinas developed his moral theory along similar lines, as did the Anglican moral theologians who are called the Caroline divines.[1] This approach in ethics is strong in the writings of Catholic popes: In Pope Leo XIII's social encyclicals, and the encyclicals of Pius XII, John XXIII, Paul VI, and John Paul II. Natural law's methodological principles are also basic to a wide range of contemporary moralists such as John Dewey, Lawrence Kohlberg, Carol Gilligan, Alasdair MacIntyre, John Connery, John Finnis, Germain Grisez, and Richard McCormick.

Both "naturalists," and "natural law" theorists share similar convictions about moral knowledge, as N.H.G. Robinson explains.[2] Both express a well established respect for reason, and acknowledge the universality of "moral awareness," the fact that moral consciousness is one of the distinctive marks of human life. They hold that morality is a self-contained phenomenon to be studied in its own right. Further, both groups are united in the traditional belief that morality—whether philosophical or religious—involves categorical absolutes that allow no alternatives. For instance, that "injustice" is the same whether one is

31

Christian or Hindu, because it is intolerable to admit the possibility of radical disagreements about primary principles, cardinal virtues, basic goods, or fundamental human rights (32).

Thus, in Kohlberg's approach to morality, scientific analysis of empirical data about teenage moral decisions will produce universally valid and objectively reliable results regardless of gender, culture, religion, or nationality. Similar organizing notions are basic to the ethics of the most important Christian thinker of the Middle Ages, Thomas Aquinas.

Aquinas's idea of reality is a creative synthesis of Aristotle's metaphysics and traditional Augustinian theology. With the scope and range of one of the great 13th century cathedrals, Thomas's ethics combines theological virtues and natural commands, reason's judgments and the will's passions. His ethical theory is a morality in which human freedom wrestles with metaphysical necessity, and insights grounded in religion (Bible, tradition), are suspended by principles based upon philosophy.

At the heart of Aquinas' moral theory are three beliefs: First, that the laws governing the "created order" participate in God's Divine law, and, therefore, our knowledge of the natural provides us with reliable (if always imperfect) data about the supernatural. Second, that, "Every aspect of reality is to be considered in relation to its true end *(telos)*, the fulfillment of which is its created purpose in being."[3] Third, that the "good" of every thing lies in the fulfillment of its *telos*, its potentiality, and "evil" consists in the fact that a thing fails to achieve or realize its goodness in not fulfilling its created *telos*.

Given these starting points, it follows that one does not have to call upon inspired insights or divine revelations to describe the *telos* of different constituents of creation. This is because (a) reason is able to "know" God's eternal laws (plans and purposes) through their effects as natural (physical, logical) laws, and (b) since all people possess reason, then, "All people are capable of knowing natural law which is universal, whether or not they are Christian" (*Ibid.*, 88).

Aquinas did not disparage Scripture. His ethic is Christocentric, and charity holds a primary place, as does the Holy Spirit. In his moral vision, eternal happiness (achieved in the contemplation of God) surpasses human nature, and can only be obtained through God's gifts of divinely infused principles (the theological virtues of faith, hope, and charity) which are not made known by reason, but by divine revelation contained in Scripture (II, I, Q.62, Art. 4). Further, divine law—as a direct revelation of God's reason and purpose—does complement natural law; it also provides a needed corrective for sinfulness and weakness, which frequently distort knowledge of this law's demands. However, unlike later Christian thinkers (Luther, Calvin, Barth), and in keeping with Paul's words in Romans (1:18–32), Aquinas does not hold that the Fall has obliterated the reasonable person's knowledge of natural law. Rather, he maintains: (a) that the natural (moral) law, if rightly understood, does not conflict with God's eternal law; and (b) that reason possesses the capacity to grasp both natural laws and created ends, and to deduce the basic "goods" which God has ordained for the human race.

This set of connections between naturally known ends, goods, and laws, provides Aquinas with the basis for his social and sexual ethic. Humans are inherently social, as Aristotle said; all of society's features—its functions and institutions—should serve the *telos* of society that is the common good. In Aquinas' sexual ethic: (i) natural goods can be derived from human nature; (ii) sexual nature is objectively oriented toward the propagation of the race, and this *telos* is its natural good; and (iii) sexual moral laws can be implied from these natural facts and logical conclusions.[4]

Similar metaphysical notions ground Thomas's economic teaching, and his opinion that "those who wage war justly aim at peace, so they are not opposed to peace, except to [an] evil peace" (I, II, Q.40, art 1).[5] Natural law morality has had strong support in Catholic circles since Aquinas.

A survey of Catholic theological texts and journals, for example, the *Irish Theological Quarterly*, shows how firmly Roman Catholic writers held this approach during the first 70 years of the 20th century. And, while there has been a strong reaction against this approach in some circles during the second half of the last century, it still has its modern champions.[6] For instance, Edward Schillebeeckx, writing about the Christian faith's ethical aspects, develops a thoroughly Thomistic position. Christianity has no ethics of its own, the Dutch theologian maintains, and is therefore open to the *humanum* that is sought by all men and women. This means that Christians do not need God as a direct foundation for their moral behavior. Morality is autonomous, and deals with the human value of individuals *etsi deus no daretur* ("as if God did not exist")—a position Schillebeeckx finds in Aquinas's *Summa Theologiae* I, II, Q.107, a.4.[7]

The Irish theologian, Enda McDonagh, has also defended the natural law tradition, although he believes that it is "misleading" to describe the moral values enshrined in created humanity and discovered in the history of human reflection as either "natural" or "legal." In

McDonagh's opinion such reflection is always carried on in the order of grace; the human is permanently grounded in God's creative saving work. Philosophical reflection on the human can never be separated from religious perceptions, both conscious and unconscious.

At the same time, McDonagh argues that Christian morality possesses some genuinely unique features, when it is described as "the way of life revealed in Christ." And it has these features because the Christian ethic is based on God's reconciling gift of sonship, a gift that is personal to each individual, yet universal in its range. The ethic is realized in different historical forms. Furthermore, to live the Christian life requires grace, the theological virtues, and the support of the Church's sacraments. In other words, it might be possible to come to know the basic principles of Christian morality without God's supernatural help, but a person cannot live that moral life without God's constant assistance.

Consequently, both historical and methodological considerations lead to the conclusion that Christian morality emerges from God's historic interventions in the past. It deals with the present that is seen always in the light of the eschatological completion of God's plan in the fullness of time (31–32).[8]

Richard McCormick's Natural Law Ethic: Reason Reflecting on the Person

The most important English-speaking religious ethicist writing consistently in the natural law "model" since World War II is Richard McCormick, one of the most powerful and prophetic voices in 20th century Roman Catholic moral theology. In spite of noticeable developments in his thought during the last 40 years (in his use of Scripture, his adoption of personalism, and his efforts to incorporate Christology), McCormick still stands squarely in the natural law tradition. As a result, as Lisa Cahill has observed, "Revisionist controversies notwithstanding, McCormick remains true to a very basic commitment that underlies the Roman Catholic tradition of moral teaching: Moral values and obligations are grounded in a moral order known by human reason reflecting on experience."[9]

As Cahill's words infer, McCormick's view of the role of the Bible in Christian ethics is radically different from John Jefferson Davis's, in spite of the fact that he has spent a great amount of his writing dealing with the relationship between Scripture's "revealed" morality and "natural law" ethics. McCormick has consistently held that Scripture does not really engage in normative ethics, and that we do not find concrete answers in revelation to the complex moral problems of the day.[10] Further, he has consistently affirmed that there is basic harmony between Scripture's "revealed" ethic and "natural law" morality. Consequently, with Schillebeeckx, he has argued that Christian morality does not add anything unique to ethics.[11]

The Bible, according to McCormick, does provide Christians with their "story," which is both the source, and the "overarching" foundation, of their morality. This "story" stands in judgment on all human meaning and actions, so that "actions which are incompatible with the story are thereby morally wrong."[12] However, as seen in his long-running debate with Stanley Hauerwas, whose approach to religious ethics can be called "narrative," McCormick firmly maintains that the Bible's stories about God, about Jesus' Incarnation, and the human condition (Adam's fall, Noah and the flood), shape the Christian's vision of life and reality. This vision can powerfully influence Christians' values and perceptions when they are involved in making moral decisions. Nevertheless, knowledge of the moral law does not directly depend on these sources.

Moreover, McCormick disagrees with Hauerwas's position that authentically Christian objections to abortion, warfare, and slavery are based on arguments that are specific to Christians. He denies Hauerwas's claim that "this rejection of abortion is in principle unavailable to human insight and reasoning without the story of revelation" (*Readings* #4, 197).[13]

For McCormick, Christian moral demands are separable from the Christian story, and make good sense in isolation from Scripture and the Christian story. In his view: (a) The Bible contains what is essentially a "human" or "natural" morality, one that is about real women and men, and one that makes sense to human reason; and (b) Christian warrants are continuous with and interpenetrate human warrants—which means that, "The Christian story does not replace the notion of 'inherent human dignity;' it supports and deepens it" (*Ibid.*, 299). Further, McCormick believes that using specifically Christian arguments in ethics will create division and confusion, and therefore, they are not appropriate in today's pluralistic societies. This is the practical, pastoral reason for the stand he takes against Hauerwas.

From his many statements on this subject, McCormick's understanding of "natural law"—for all its updating—accords with Robinson's summary of the traditional theory's three distinctive features: (a) the law is derived from the *nature* of man; (b) it is rationally derived without the aid of revelation and is thereby able to command universal assent; (c) it serves as a foundation for the "special requirements" of Christian ethics which are seen as supplemental or as a "second story" built upon the natural law's demands.[14]

"Reason informed by faith" is a dominant *motif* in McCormick's ethics. By this he means neither reason replaced by faith, nor reason without faith, but the faculty of reason shaped by faith, in such a way that this shaping takes the form of perspectives, themes, and insights associated with the Christian story.[15] Writing in 1989 on "Theology and Bioethics" in *The Hastings Center Report,* McCormick argues that the more profound the faith, the greater and more explicit the Christian consciousness; and the more explicit the consciousness, the more that Christian faith: (a) *protects* oneself and others; (b) *disposes* one to work for justice, to attend the poor, to accept dependence; and (c) *directs,* shapes consciousness, and informs reason.[16] Thus, theology will influence bioethics in important ways. "Its function is not a direct originating influence on concrete moral judgments at the essential level . . . but on 'morally relevant insights,' in the words of Franz Bockle" (10). For McCormick, the outcome of such an "informing" is a "distinct —though not utterly mysterious—way of viewing the world and ourselves and of hierarchizing values" (10). It will result in a distinctively Christian *concern*.[17] The Christian religion colors one's vision and heart, but it does not provide distinctive norms or rules.

A second central criterion in McCormick's ethic is basic to Vatican II's morality, and to personalism, namely, "the human person integrally and adequately considered."[18] When McCormick turns to moral decision-making, and resolving medical dilemmas (his primary area of application), he does not speak about the "illative" sense, or "knowledge of co-naturality," as earlier 20th century natural law thinkers such as Etienne Gilson and Jacques Maritain did. He does not give a major place to conscience as John Henry Newman did. McCormick's approach involves logic, deduction and induction, analysis and synthesis, grasping connections, and carefully weighing arguments in the light of objective criteria. Over the years, through working closely with physicians and philosophers, McCormick has examined the foundations of Catholic moral theology like a surgeon. At the same time he has sought to find arguments and language that make the Church's teaching more convincing. Thus, he has concluded that surrogacy is immoral because "marital exclusivity" ought to include the genetic, gestational, and rearing dimensions of parenthood, and separating these dimensions too easily creates a subtle diminishment of the human person.[19] In the face of what he considers examples of "biologism and vitalism," McCormick has contended that Nancy Cruzan should have been allowed to die, because of the "uselessness"of her existence in a persistent vegetative state, and the obvious lack of genuine "benefits" from providing her with fluids.[20] He has used "potential for human relationships" as a central criterion for making decisions about letting severely handicapped newborns live or die.[21]

Rather than making decisions directly on the basis of such considerations as the Bible, Christ's compassion, or the care that should be shown to "images of God" (as Allen Verhey has done in writing about euthanasia), McCormick has consistently looked at these issues in terms of his updated "natural law" approach, and he has resolved these problems in terms of faith-informed assessments of the person's purpose, dignity, and well-being.

The Natural Law Model: An Assessment

McCormick's greatest contribution to natural law ethics, according to Cahill, is "to tie it more realistically to human experience and to individual and communal discretion. . . . His distinctive position on the relation between faith and ethics affirms the ability of reason reflecting on experience to grasp essential moral obligations, but also much more self-consciously sets reasonable reflection within a life-perspective shaped by faith" (Cahill, *Ibid.*, 101–102).[22] McCormick's ethic contains much to admire—it is open, engaging, and contemporary. His approach makes it possible to reach both those who have no religion, and those who possess religious convictions quite different from Christianity. Like Aquinas's ethic, his "mixed deontology" leaves much to discuss, in particular his basic convictions: (a) That laws, ends, and potentialities associated with the human person are the basis of morality; (b) that faith-informed reason can establish objective, universal norms of "essential" morality, as well as make reliable "individual" decisions from its applications of "norms" associated with the human person; and (c) that this "natural" morality is identical with the fundamentals of Christian (i.e., Biblical) morality. There are other—more difficult—issues as well. Modern thought has abandoned Aquinas's teleological cosmology. His worldview now belongs to science's scrap heap, along with Dante's pre-Copernican model of the universe. Today, there is no possibility of a consensus about "human nature," and chaos theorists and postmodern psychologists have moved well beyond Leslie Stevenson's seven familiar descriptions.[23] The natural law approach suffers problems associated with its ancient and complex heritage, the fact that it has its roots in Aristotle's ethics, Hellenistic politics, Stoic cosmology, Roman law, not to mention Ambrose's morality, and Augustine's ecclesiology. Further, although the United Nations Declaration on Human Rights canonizes a set of generally agreed upon rights, it is difficult, nevertheless, for religious communities and political societies to articulate universal moral laws, as the recent community discussions about contraception, abortion, homosexuality, and euthanasia have shown.

There are more problems. Contemporary Roman Catholic and Protestant moral theology have taken a strong stand against naturalistic ethics. Consequently, Catholic ethicists are moving at speed to establish moral theories based on God's grace, and Christ's Revelation. Also, while somewhat moderated in McCormick's hands, the natural law approach emphasizes reason, and objective, universal rules—themes currently out of favor with feminists, as we have seen. Furthermore, the social sciences have put forward convincing reasons to support the view that the structures of morality, built into culture and experience, are not static laws constitutive of "nature," but dynamic and changing norms (different from culture to culture), generated by social experiences in history.[24] As well, Karl Rahner's theology has moved Catholic ethics toward existentialism and situationism, toward seeing morality in terms of individuals and specific situations, and accepting Ignatius Loyola's process of life-choice, namely, discernment.[25] Younger Roman Catholic ethicists trained in the social sciences have a greater sense of historicity than McCormick, and they have little difficulty accepting the position that "Morality is, quintessentially, the person as person, i.e., the person in his or her enduring choice 'with respect to the totality of existence, its meaning and its direction.'"[26]

There is a final and hard-to-overcome problem with this approach. As N.H.G. Robinson notes, "If God was in Christ reconciling the world to himself, that reconciliation is very imperfectly portrayed by the idea of a supplement" (303).[27] From the beginning, Christianity has proclaimed that there is something "special" about Jesus—that he is the "son of man," a "prophet" in the tradition of Moses and Elijah, Isaiah's "suffering servant," and the Logos. Once a person accepts these creedal beliefs about Jesus, it is difficult for Christians to accept that their morality, described in terms of "following Christ," means nothing more than living according to reason's perceptions of human nature, and that Jesus' moral demands add nothing really new.

The Natural Law Approach: Future Prospects

Given the Catholic Church's long association with this approach, this moral "model" will have its supporters well into the future, in spite of its abandonment by mainstream moral philosophy. Because Aquinas holds such a significant place in the history of theology, and his thought has a definite place in the recently published *Catechism of the Catholic Church,* natural law morality has a guaranteed future. Its emphasis on reason's ability to provide objective, universal ethical principles will always attract naturalists working in the physical and human sciences.

For those who enjoy marching to a different drummer, there will always be appeal in making moral decisions on the basis of the "finality" inherent in life's dynamisms, and on the basis of the "meaning" and "purpose" in nature's dynamisms and structures.

NOTES

[1] For their contributions to natural law theory, N.H.D. Robinson, *The Groundwork of Christian Ethics* (London: Collins, 1971), 302, 303.

[2] N.H.G. Robinson, *Ibid.,* 31ff.

[3] J. Philip Wogaman, *Ibid.,* 84.

[4] N.H.G. Robinson, *Ibid.,* 37.

[5] For further on these subjects, J. Philip Wogaman, *Christian Ethics: A Historical Introduction* (Louisville, KY: Westminster John Knox, 1993), 90–94; George V. Lobo, *Guide to Christian Living: A New Compendium of Moral Theology,* (Westminster, MD: Christian Classics, 1985), 5–7, 10–11, 149–150.

[6] The reasons for this reaction are summarized by Gregory Baum in "Catholic Sexual Morality: A New Start," *The Ecumenist* 11, 3 (March–April 1973), 33–38, at 35–36.

[7] Edward Schillebeeckx, *ON CHRISTIAN FAITH: The Spiritual, Ethical, and Political Dimensions* (New York: Crossroad Publishing, 1987).

[8] For McDonagh's valuable analysis of the relationship between Christian morality and natural law, Enda McDonagh, "The Natural Law and the Law of Christ" in *Invitation and Response: Essays in Christian Moral Theology* (New York: Sheed & Ward, 1972), 22–37.

[9] Lisa Sowle Cahill, "Richard A. McCormick: Reason and Faith in Post-Vatican II Catholic Ethics," in Allen Verhey and Stephen E. Lammers (Editors), *Theological Voices in Medical Ethics* (Grand Rapids: Eerdmans, 1993), 78–105, at 81–82.

[10] Richard A. McCormick, "Notes on Moral Theology," in *Theological Studies* (1977), 628.

[11] Richard A. McCormick, "Christianity and Morality," *Catholic Mind* 75, (October 1977), 17–29. Charles Curran also supports this position, cf. Charles Curran, "Is There a Distinctively Christian Social Ethic?" in *Metropolis: Christian Presence and Responsibility* (Notre Dame: Fides, 1970).

[12] Richard A. McCormick, "Theology and Bioethics: Christian Foundations," in *Theology and Bioethics: Exploring the Foundations and Frontiers,* Earl Shelp (Editor), (Dordrecht: D. Reidel, 1985), 95ff.

[13] For an analysis of this debate, Michael E. Allsopp and Edward R. Sunshine, "Speaking Morally: The Thirty Year Debate between Richard A. McCormick and Stanley Hauerwas," *Irish Theological Quarterly* 63, 1 (1998), 51–64.

[14]For these, and other important observations about current discussions of natural law, N.H.G. Robinson, op. cit., 302–307.

[15]On this subject, Richard A. McCormick, "Bioethics and Method: Where do we start?" *Theology Digest* 29, 303–318.

[16]Richard McCormick, "Theology and Bioethics," *Hastings Center Report* 19 (1989), 5–10.

[17]On this subject, Richard A. McCormick *Notes on Moral Theology, Ibid.*, 296–303, at 303.

[18]For one analysis of this principle, Richard A. McCormick, *Health and Medicine in the Catholic Tradition* (New York: Crossroads, 1984), 15–19

[19]Richard A. McCormick, "Surrogacy: A Catholic Perspective," in *Corrective Vision: Explorations in Moral Theology* (Kansas City: Sheed & Ward, 1994), 201–209.

[20]Richard A. McCormick, "The Case of Nancy Cruzan: A Reflection," in *Corrective Vision*, Ibid., 219–224.

[21]Richard A. McCormick, "To Save or Let Die," *America*, 130 (July 13, 1974), 6–10. Revised in "Saving Defective Infants: Options for Life or Death," *America*, 139 (1983), 313–317.

[22]Christian feminists, (as we have seen,) also build their morality on the basis of reflection on experience. However, feminists give special authority to women's experience (African-American, marginalized Hispanic women). Their reflection is frequently communal or group, and there is no expectation of universal norms, no demand for universals in their practical ethics, as in McCormick's. Historicity, "constructive relativism," finitude, change, subjectivity, creativity, particularity, autonomy, interdependence, liberation—these are features prized not spurned by feminists. cf. Sharon D. Welch, *Feminist Ethics of Risk* (Minneapolis: Fortress, 1990).

[23]Leslie Stevenson, *Seven Theories of Human Nature* (New York: Oxford University Press, 1987).

[24]For the influence of the role of history on natural law see, Joseph Fuchs, *Natural Law* (New York: Sheed & Ward, 1965).

[25]On this subject, Michael E. Allsopp, "Karl Rahner's Formal-Existentialist Ethics: A Study," *Australasian Catholic Record* 50, 2 (April 1973), 113–129; and 50, 3 (October 1973), 331–339.

[26]Norbert Rigali, "Christ and Morality" in *The Distinctiveness of Christian Ethics, Readings in Moral Theology #2*, edited by Charles E. Curran, and Richard A. McCormick (New York: Paulist Press, 1980), 111–120.

[27]There appear to be some developments between McCormick's early and more recent statements on these subjects, although he still seems to maintain his basic understandings. For further on McCormick's ethics see, Michael E. Allsopp, "Deontic and Epistemic Authority in Roman Catholic Ethics: The Case of Richard McCormick," *Christian Bioethics* 2, 1 (1996), 97–113; Michael E. Allsopp, "The Role of Scripture in Richard A. McCormick's Ethics," *Chicago Studies* 35, 2 (August 1996), 185–196. Also, Gerald J. Hughes, "Natural Law," in *Christian Ethics: An Introduction* edited by Bernard Hoose (London: Cassell, 1998), 47–56; N.H.G. Robinson, op. cit., 31–54, 302–307; James Gustafson, *Protestant and Roman Catholic Ethics* (Chicago: University of Chicago Press, 1978), 6–12; "The Natural Moral Law," in George V. Lobo, op. cit., 168–197.

CHAPTER 4

Situation Ethics

S ituation ethics is a child of the 1960s. A widespread trend rather than a tightly unified system, it is a reaction against the "old" morality (just as "impressionism" was a broad reaction against the "old" art). Both European and American situationism is a "model" of morality that embodies the spirit and enthusiasm of the social and intellectual revolutions of the times. Along with Harvey Cox's *The Secular City* (1965), and John A. T. Robinson's *Honest to God* (1963), Paul Lehmann's *Ethics in a Christian Context* (1963), and Joseph Fletcher's *Situation Ethics* (1966) spoke to a generation of Christians that felt it was living at a turning point in world and cultural history.

Situation Ethics: Overview

"Situation ethics is a utilitarian or consequentialist ethics, motivated by concern for human well-being, decisionally flexible in method and guided in its judgments by the greatest good realizable rather than by adhering to prefabricated norms or moral rules," Joseph Fletcher wrote in 1979.[1] Given the wide support of consequentialism in Anglo-American moral philosophy, and what we find in Fletcher's major works, for example, *Morals and Medicine* (1954), *Moral Responsibility: Situation Ethics at Work* (1967), *The Ethics of Genetic Control* (1974), *Humanhood: Essays in Biomedical Ethics* (1979), plus his frequent essays in the *Hastings Center Report,* and his contributions to the *Encyclopedia of Bioethics* (1979), his original formulation of Christian ethics must be considered an inherently powerful and widely appealing approach. It incorporates a number of features that any serious Christian ethicist must respect. Whatever critics say about its shortcomings, Situation ethics is a model of social and individual ethics that has raised crucial methodological and epistemological issues in Christian morality. As Waldo Beach says in *Christian Ethics in the Protestant Tradition* (1988): "It has made a major contribution to the development of Christian ethics."[2]

The forward to Fletcher's bestseller *Situation Ethics* provides us with a quick summary of the book's themes and insights, its distinctive tone and range.[3] Fletcher's citations from G. E. Moore, William James, William Temple, and Paul Tillich underline his acceptance of "consequentialism" as defined by Elizabeth Anscombe in her essay "Modern Moral Philosophy" (1958); they highlight his emphasis on the pragmatic, on love as the ultimate and absolute law in concrete situations. Fletcher's forward also shows us his debt to E.E. Cummings in calling his ethics a "*non*system" (11); to Paul Ramsey for his valuable assessments (16); to Harvard Divinity School, Kenyon College, International Christian University in Tokyo; to his wife, and to students in American medical, business, and theological schools (16).

Early in the book, we are aware of Fletcher's emphasis on ethics in terms of decision-making rather than as a guide for one's life (11), on method rather than system (11–12), his conviction that this approach is really not "new" either in method or in content (12–13); and, that as a method, the roots of Situation ethics lie securely in the classical tradition of western Christian morality (13). Finally, Fletcher defends his theological framework (15), his use of the word "love"(15), and acknowledges Paul Ramsey's judgments that Situation ethics is both personalistic and contextual (14)—features that will be examined below, as well as when looking at other models of Christian morality examined in this book.

In order to better understand Fletcher's ethics, it is important to examine several foundational aspects. First, the term "situation" (or "context") is variously defined. However, the term, taken from modern European philosophy, means the specific result of the space, time, and other factors in which an agent is always involved when making a moral decision. "Situation" embodies the modern insight that each of us is always and inextricably living and acting within a particular framework. Thus, "situation" includes such aspects as the physical, biological, social, historical, cultural, psychological, religious and moral—what traditional ethics calls the "circumstances" of the human act.

For situationists, however, these features are not simply "accidents," but the "essentials" of morality; they change the way we look at and decide ethical issues. They are always unique and unrepeatable in reality, not open to generalization. They are the intrinsic determinants of the morality of any action, and the locus of God's work and will in the world.

Secondly, while those who have taken courses in contemporary moral theories will be familiar with the material, it is useful to recall the main tenets of the "utilitarian" theory of ethics, because Fletcher consciously developed an "Act-Utilitarian" moral theory. Utilitarianism, the most prominent consequentialist-based ethical theory, affirms, in the words that Fletcher quotes from William James, "There is but one unconditional commandment, which is that we should seek incessantly, with fear and trembling, so to vote and to act as to bring about the very largest total universe of good we can see." The intellectual roots of the two modern forms of this optimizing moral theory, that is, "Rule-Utilitarianism" (Richard Brandt), and "Act-Utilitarianism" (Joseph Fletcher), lie in the writings of David Hume (1711–1776), Jeremy Bentham (1748–1832), and John Stuart Mill (1806–1873), each of whom gave support to the principle that "that action is best, which procures the greatest happiness for the greatest numbers; and that, worst, which, in like manner, occasions misery," to quote one of the earliest formulations of the principle of utility.[4]

As James Rachels, John Rawls, Bernard Williams and others make clear in discussing this approach to ethics, utilitarians emphasize egalitarianism, and the impartial weighing of possible alternatives; theirs is an ethics of decisions and public affairs. They claim that the rightness or wrongness of human actions are exclusively a function of the goodness or badness of the consequences (short-term or long-term), resulting directly or indirectly from these actions. A person ought to act so as to produce the greatest balance of good over evil, everyone considered.

Act-utilitarians have no sympathy for the notion that some actions are always intrinsically wrong. Rather, they support the view that an action (such as lying) may be wrong in one set of circumstances yet right in another, that the morality of an action is a function of the situation's impact on its outcomes.

Fletcher's original combination of utilitarianism, pragmatism, situational thinking, as well as mainstream Christian ethics, reflects his ministry in the Episcopal Church. It also reflects his years as professor of pastoral theology and his roles in organizations such as the Euthanasia Society of America, Planned Parenthood of America, and the American Sociological Society. All these forces result in the following set of summary conclusions about moral method and how we come to know right and wrong: A situationist will see each moral decision as the act of entering actively into each unique and specific decision-making situation ("Should *I* treat aggressively *this* severely impaired infant of *this* mother and *this* family?"); he or she will be fully armed with the ethical maxims of his or her religious, cultural and legal community, and its heritage; and he or she will treat this data with respect as illuminators of his or her problems.

In the case of a *Christian* situationist (those of other faiths or philosophies will have their own visions, laws, and maxims), he or she will be guided throughout the decision making process by the one absolute and universal ethical principle of Christianity, "Thou shalt love thy neighbor as thyself"—which means that one's final decision will be based not upon what is *natural* or *scriptural,* but on an assessment ("careful calculation on a wide range") of which course of action is the most loving, concerned, and human-helping in this concrete situation. This is seen in Fletcher's now famous Mrs. Bergmeier case, arguably the most discussed case in modern ethics (Appendix, 165).

We find Fletcher's views about traditional Christian ethics throughout *Situation Ethics*. For instance, "Judaism, Catholicism, Protestantism—all major Western religious traditions have been legalistic" (18). "Situation ethics goes part of the way with natural law, by accepting reason as the instrument of moral judgment, while rejecting the notion that the good is 'given' in the nature of things, objectively. It goes part of the way with Scriptural law by accepting revelation as the source of the norm while rejecting all 'revealed' norms or laws but the one command—to love God in the neighbor. The situationist follows a moral law or violates it according to love's need" (26). "It is necessary to insist that situation ethics is willing to make full and respectful use of principles, to be treated as maxims but not as laws or precepts. It might be called 'principled relativism'"(31).

The greater part of Fletcher's easy to read and engaging book (57–145) deals with five propositions about love, Fletcher's highest good or *summum bonum*. Here we find the author's summary defense of his belief that: "Only one thing is intrinsically good, namely, love: Nothing else at all" (68); "the ruling norm of Christian decision is love: Nothing else" (86); "Love and justice are the same, for justice is love distributed, nothing else" (99); "love wills the neighbor's good whether we like him or not" (119); "only the end justifies the means: Nothing else" (133); "love's decisions are made situationally, not prescriptively" (145).

Situation Ethics does not provide the type of systematic presentation of moral theory that we find in G.E. Moore's *Principia Ethica*, although it has many of the literary features (original voice, quick pace, and articulate speech), that we have already examined in looking at Sharon D. Welch's *A Feminist Ethics of Risk*. Rather than tightly constructed analyses, Fletcher gives us lucid, pithy statements—notecards—which provide us with clear outlines of his approach. He gives readers brief sketches of his justifications. In Fletcher's eyes, his ethics provides a middle path between the yoke of moral "legalism" that eventually overburdens its supporters, and the abandon of "antinomianism" that advances chaos and anarchy (17–39). It aims at a "contextual appropriateness—not the 'good' or the 'right' but the *fitting*" (27–28).

Fletcher's form of situation ethics is based upon the insight that "circumstances alter cases—i.e., that in actual problems of conscience situational variables e.g., a patient's physical condition, the resources on hand in this ICU, change our decisions; and (second) that these variables are to be weighed as heavily as the normative or 'general' constants," for example, the norms of medical ethics—autonomy, beneficence, and justice (29). In taking this stand, Fletcher's method has a lot in common with a moral "model," not examined in this book because it is less popular or influential, (casuistry). This is an approach which also tries to adduce experientially, not deduce, moral norms that are held tentatively and developed case by case.

A careful reading shows that Fletcher has no real dislike for rules or principles—as he has been accused—unless they are hardened into laws (32). Further, Fletcher sees his theory as an expression of American *pragmatism*, in that it turns away from abstraction and turns toward the concrete, toward facts, actions, and power (43). It is *relativistic* (but it does have one absolute—love). Like James Gustafson's theocentric ethics, Fletcher's situation ethics denies theological naturalism in which reason deduces faith propositions and religious moral norms from human experience or natural phenomena. Instead it advocates theological *positivism*, i.e., a careful thinking about life and reality that is supported by and based upon religious faith; a Christian ethics that starts by positing faith in a God who is love, and then reasons out what fidelity to that God's call to love requires in any situation.

Finally, Fletcher's ethics, like Louis Janssens' *Personalism* (which has an influence on Richard McCormick), presupposes that morality means putting people at the center of our concerns, not things; being responsible to persons and to personal relationships—it grounds ethics on significant human relationships, as W.D. Ross does in his deonto-logical ethics (50–52). For Fletcher, Jesus taught a situational kind of freedom from moral law, an ethics in which morals were made for man not man for morals. Jesus was a Jew whose morality centered on love instead of law. Fletcher writes, "I personally would adopt nearly all the norms or action-principles ordinarily held in Christian ethics. I refuse, on the other hand, to treat their norms as idols—as divinely finalized" (*Debate*, 252).

James Gustafson's theocentric ethics is grounded on the question "What is God calling us to do?" Fletcher's ethics is based upon the question, "How do we know the loving thing to do?" And this because, in Fletcher's mind, we do not and cannot know what God is doing, because "the Christian has no inside track cognitively" (254). Further, Situation ethics does not deny the role of grace in morality, nor does it eliminate sin (256–257). Neither does it ignore the Church's role or the authority of Scripture. Fletcher's sources are Revelation and Christian writers. His ethics is a religious ethics in which faith comes first, and reason, while vital in decision-making, cannot bridge the gap between empirical facts and religious beliefs. It is a moral theory in which conscience has a central place (*Situation Ethics,* 52–55).

Finally, Fletcher has maintained that his ethics is based upon two guidelines from Paul: "The written code kills, but the Spirit gives life" (2 Corinthians 3:6), and "For the whole law is fulfilled in one word, 'You shall love your neighbor as yourself' (Galatians 5:14)," as he states in *Situation Ethics* (30). A fact finding, empirically tempered yet personalist and religious ethic for the present, his method has, nevertheless, its eschatological meaning.

All these Christian aspects of Fletcher's ethics are seen in his closing summary statement: "Christian ethics or moral theology is not a scheme of living according to a code but a continuous effort to relate love to a world of relativities through a casuistry obedient to love; its constant task is to work out the strategy and tactics of love, for Christ's sake" (158).

Situation Ethics: Weighing Its Worth

Fletcher's ethics is widely discussed in *The Situation Ethics Debate*, edited by Harvey Cox, in N.H.G. Robinson's *The Groundwork of Christian Ethics* (1971), John Macquarrie's *Three Issues in Ethics* (1970), William Barclay's *Christian Ethics for Today* (1971), and more recently in Roger H. Crook's *An Introduction to Christian Ethics* (1990), as well as in scores of journal essays. Situation ethics has been condemned as "simply another example of the rebellion of fallen man against his Creator" (*Debate*, 87); it has been praised as a theory that has contributed immeasurably to the "democratization" of theological conversation (*Debate,* 11–17).

Situation Ethics has been called a "watershed in the history of moral theology" (73), and positively compared with Carl Rogers' *Counseling and Psychotherapy,* another popular book that provides discussion, and highly constructive controversy (*Debate,* 53). On the other hand, the book has been called anti-Christian, corrupting, and a parent to an ethics of improvisation and normlessness by evangelicals and conservatives.[5]

Before looking at these criticisms, both favorable and unfavorable, a word about the formal and material criteria for assessing any moral theory or ethical model. As mentioned in the Introduction, a carefully articulated moral theory provides a framework within which we can reflect upon the rightness or wrongness of human behavior; it allows us to evaluate an agent's moral judgments and character. Therefore, while not all theories are equally coherent or complete, nor all as well expressed or finely polished, to be given the status of a "theory" means that there has been some effort to engage in the speculative and the theoretical. The theorist has attempted to provide some organization of methodological rules and epistemological (truth) principles, and to present some systematic analysis and argument about morality, the right and the good, and how we know them. Further, those who engage in developing moral theories have some responsibility to explain and defend their presuppositions, as well as their more immediate affirmations. Although a theorist can legitimately assume that readers are educated and informed, he or she should neither insult readers' intelligence nor leave them grasping in the dark for vital information about the salient features of his or her theory.

Such a theory will be internally consistent, and reconcilable with our experience of morality; it will provide effective guidance, especially in those areas where there is ambiguity. Further, although neoconservatives and liberals will disagree about these criteria, a theory or model of Christian ethics will embody some specific material features that allows it to meet the demands inherent in the claim that it is *Christian.* And it will be *Christian* to the extent that it satisfies the criteria mentioned by Avery Dulles in his *Models of the Church.*

On the basis of its internal features, and its enduring and wide impact upon Christian ethics, Fletcher's moral method must score high. It is clearly and appealingly expressed; it is coherent, complete, simple, and practical. It possesses the ability to justify and explain; and generated numerous insights. His theory is consistent, reconcilable with moral experience, and it provides moral guidance in cases filled with ambiguity. Unlike W.D. Ross's deontological ethics, situation ethics possesses a guiding principle for resolving moral dilemmas. Furthermore, situation ethics speaks to the "silent majority" of Anglo-American philosophers and students of ethics; its utilitarian-type of decision-making appeals to "nonphilosopers" who think about moral issues, as well as to those involved in policy-making and public affairs—as college teachers of business ethics, and those who have conducted medical ethics courses for nurses have found. Situation ethics like Ayn Rand's Objectivism resonates with American individualists.

Among the major negative criticisms of Fletcher's ethics, one finds the following. While John Macquarrie supports Fletcher's reactions against legalism in Protestant and Roman Catholic ethics, he is critical of the stress that Situation ethics' places on the uniqueness of each act, and its dislike of rules, customs, and habits (*Three Issues*, 32–33). He considers that Fletcher's method "breaks up the moral life into separate acts in such a way as to deny the reality of a unitary personal self that grows and deepens through its successive experiences" (33). It subverts any idea of a moral community (33–34), and it suffers from the vice of subjectivism (34–35). Further, Macquarrie considers situation ethics to be unrealistic in its optimistic view of Christians (35). He is critical of Fletcher's unclear statements about a "situation" (35), and supports Bernard Haring's opinion that Fletcher's concept of love is "structureless," a view also expressed by James Gustafson (*Debate*, 78–79).

N.H.G. Robinson has expressed concern about Fletcher's utilitarianism and relativism.[6] "If a comprehensive relativism which permits love as the only absolute is taken seriously—and this is what Fletcher seriously means—it confronts the moral agent with an unanswerable question, and in the absence of an answer it throws the gates wide open to caprice and impulse, to sentimentalism and fanaticism, to naturalism and actualism of one kind or another," Robinson writes (249). Further, Robinson believes that clarity of thought requires more attention to the well-known distinction between deontological and teleological ethics than Fletcher is prepared to give when he says that "one's 'duty' is to seek the goal of the most love possible in every situation and one's 'goal' is to obey the command to do just that!" (249–250).

The fact that Fletcher's ethics is act-utilitarian means that it must face the criticisms raised against this theory by W.D. Ross, J.L. Mackie, John Finnis, Tom Regan, and Richard Brandt. These criticisms are that it has no room for absolute moral rights nor the inherent value of individuals; and that human actions have no inherent value, but are like cups containing different liquids. As well, it must face the additional concerns that Samuel Scheffler and Iris Murdoch have raised about act-utilitarianism's demoralizing demand for maximization of results, and its lack of realism, since there are few people who can commit themselves to always doing the loving—self-sacrificing-thing. There are fewer still who will live by the rule that says, "Do always what will achieve the most good for the greatest number—yourself included."

Is Fletcher's method adequate in terms of its grasp of *Christian* features? Does his approach preserve an adequate number of the elements of *Christian* ethics? In spite of Fletcher's claims to have developed a Christian personalism, his ethics can be faulted for its reductionism: It reduces Christ's ethics simply to his command to love. It also reduces all the Bible's rules and commands to a single absolute. For the Evangelical ethicist, John Jefferson Davis, the fundamental difficulty with Fletcher's ethics is its absence of any definite criterion for what consitutes a "loving" course of action in any situation.[7] As well, his method gives a too limited role to the church community, and too much autonomy to the individual in its naive view of the individual's sense of moral responsibility.

"Situation ethics is built on an apostate view of human nature and human sin," according to another conservative critic, Harvie Conn (58). It gives the impression that humans are rational and selfless. In William Barclay's opinion "situation ethics presents us with a terrifying degree of freedom."[8] Further, situation ethics reduces morality simply to decision making and says too little about an ethics of character and moral development. While Fletcher's ethics is theocentric (it takes its central principle from God's Word), and it rests upon Christ's love command, one finds few references to the Spirit and to the sacraments in his work. "The situationist is liable to forget quite simply the grace of God," Barclay writes (83). Like many moral theories, situation ethics is Pelagian in its emphasis on human reason and will—the inherent goodness of humans.

Also situation ethics implies that the Judeo-Christian story makes little difference in medical or business ethics: Christian morality becomes the loving result of an individual's responsible decisions —nothing more. This problem was addressed in the Vatican's 1956 instruction on the early European expressions of situation ethics that saw the decisive and ultimate norm of morality in "a certain intimate judgment and light of the mind of each individual, by means of which, in the concrete situation in which he is placed, he learns what he ought to do."[9] For these critics, there is more to Christian morality than making loving decisions; the Church's creed, and its vision of reality, cannot be reduced to Christ's love command.

Conclusion: An Anti-Theory for Non-Academics

This model of Christian ethics is easily grasped and quickly understood; it resonates with nonphilosophers. Joseph Fletcher's work will be long remembered when the ethical theories of other Christian writers have been forgotten either because they are too obscure in expression or too impractical in application. His theory does possess the weaknesses that critics find in all act-utilitarian ethical models; it is also clearly minimalist in its Christian doctrinal features.

Nevertheless, Fletcher's situation ethics has made a major impact upon Christian ethical theory; it possesses strengths that one does not find in some of the other models that we are examining. Whatever the shortcomings we see in Fletcher's approach: its over-optimism with regard to humans, and its reduction of Christian morality to loving actions, this approach has earned the loyal support of millions of contemporary Christians working in business, medicine, and human services, because situation ethics works. It provides today's busy physicians, nurses, and teachers with rationally defensible answers to life's complex moral problems; it is pragmatic and practical.

NOTES

[1] Joseph Fletcher, "Situation Ethics," in *Encyclopedia of Bioethics*, First Edition, edited by Warren T. Reich (New York: Free Press, 1978), 1, 421–424.

[2] Waldo Beach, *Christian Ethics in the Protestant Tradition* (Atlanta: John Knox Press, 1988), 45.

[3] Joseph Fletcher, *Situation Ethics: The New Morality* (Philadelphia: Westminster Press, 1966).

[4] On this subject, John Rawls on "Classical Utilitarianism," in *A Theory of Justice*, chapter 1, (Cambridge, MA: Harvard University Press, 1971).

[5] Harvie M. Conn, *Contemporary World Theology: A Layman's Guidebook* (Phillipsburg, NJ: Presbyterian and Reformed Publishing Company, 1973), 53–58.

[6] N. H. G. Robinson, *The Groundwork of Christian Ethics* (London: Collins, 1971).

[7] John Jefferson Davis, *Evangelical Ethics: Issues Facing the Church Today* (Phillipsburg, NJ: Presbyterian and Reformed Publishing Company, 1985), 13.

[8] William Barclay, *Christian Ethics for Today* (San Francisco: Harper & Row, 1984) 80.

[9] On the background of Fletcher's ethics, John G. Milhaven and David J. Casey, "Introduction to the Theological Background of the New Morality," *Theological Studies*, 28 (1967), 213–244. For the Vatican's statements, *Acta Apostolicae Sedis (A.A.S.), 44 (1952), 270–78; 413–19; 48 (1956), 144–145.* Also, Michael E. Allsopp, "Joseph Fletcher's *Situation Ethics*: Twenty-Five Years after the Storm," *Irish Theological Quarterly*, 56, 3 (1990), 170–190.

CHAPTER 5

Theocentric Ethics

James Gustafson's "theocentric ethics" belongs to a moral tradition with a long history. In a sense, all Jewish, Christian, and Muslim moralities are "God-centered." However, some religious moral theories focus more specifically on the deity rather than on such reference points as natural law, or Sacred Scripture. In these theories, "God" not "Creation" is the source or dominant theme of ethics. In this century, Karl Barth developed a specifically "theocentric" ethics,[1] while Emil Brunner identified moral "goodness" with what God does, and argued that the Christian ethic reveals the Good, the one really and truly Good. "No one has a claim on a man, or on a people, save God alone," Brunner wrote. "And this claim permeates all the relationships of life. It is the only valid norm."[2]

More recently, the American theologian John Howard Yoder, best known for his defense of Christian pacifism, has articulated an ethics that flows out of a Barthian vision of God's *kenotic* ("self-emptying") way of love and success.[3] And in Roman Catholic circles, Pope John Paul II's morality is clearly "theocentric," as we see from the *theological* argument based on a couple's "cooperation with God's creative power" which the pope has used to demonstrate the Church's stand on contraception.[4]

However, the American Protestant theologian, James Gustafson, Henry R. Luce Professor of Humanities and Comparative Studies at Emory University, prior to his retirement late in the 1990s, is the best known recent proponent of a "God-centered" moral theory. Gustafson, who stands with Notre Dame's Richard A. McCormick as one of the most prophetic voices in 20th century moral theology, was one of the first theologians to address medical ethics issues in the 1960s. He also wrote major studies on Roman Catholic and Protestant ethics, on such topics as the place of Scripture in Christian ethics, and the role of the church as a community of moral discourse. While practical and pastoral, Gustafson's most important work deals with moral methodology, and with articulating an up to date Christian ethical theory which is thoroughly religious, because it is shaped by specifically *theological* convictions.

51

This chapter will examine the foundations of Gustafson's theory, its religious roots and historical connections, and it will provide a summary and assessment of the theory's original features, its strengths and weaknesses. Both Protestants and Catholics have much to gain from Gustafson's highly readable, future oriented "theocentric" moral model, which is rich in possibilities.

Theocentric Ethics: James Gustafson's Approach

Tourists seeking travel directions in Ireland are occasionally told, "Well, I wouldn't go there from here." They are reminded that one's starting point has a major impact on how one reaches one's destination. Gustafson's ethics emphasizes orientation; it also appreciates the importance of perspective, a theme crucial to the climax of the musical *Camelot,* where the wizard Merlin teaches a dejected King Arthur to see things through the eyes of a bird—a skill which dramatically alters Arthur's values and perceptions. Gustafson's theocentric ethics causes similar changes in our orientation and judgment. Because of his convictions about creation, culture, the Almighty, and, most of all, the role of religion in shaping morality,[5] Gustafson's theory forces us to construe reality in new ways: To think less about individual happiness and more about cosmic good; to discern not what we, but what God is calling and empowering us to be and to do; to broaden the focus of morality, and to study the patterns and processes of interdependence (physical, social, cultural) in which humans, animals, and inanimate creatures participate.

For this independent and creative theologian, moral philosophy can lead humans toward beauty, truth, and goodness. However, a *religious* ethics—the task of the moral theologian—flows from religious sources and builds upon religious realities; it looks at life from God's perspective rather than a human (secular, rational) point of view. Consequently, it calls humans to take hard roads, and seek long-term perspectives.

On the basis of what we find throughout Gustafson's writings on religious ethics, in particular, his two volume *Ethics from a Theocentric Perspective* (1994, 1981), the major features of this moral theory result from deep convictions and reasoned analyses about the shape of Christian morality.[6] Gustafson's controlling notions that "religion qualifies morality," and that Christian ethics should be "God-centered" rather than "man-centered," result from: (a) His study of the history of ethics, and (b) his religious, pastoral, and personal convictions.

Philosophical and Religious Ethics: The Differences for Gustafson

In his analysis of the methodology of Vatican's 1975 *Declaration on Certain Questions Concerning Sexual Ethics*, the Catholic moral theologian William E. May (Catholic University of America), shows that the document echoes the thought of Catholic natural law thinkers and personalists, such as, Dietrich von Hilderbrand. In May's judgment, the papal letter reaches specific conclusions about premarital sex, adultery, and homosexuality from an examination of the human significance of sexuality.[7] In keeping with what is best called the "classical" mentality, May argues that God's "unchanging truths and laws can be known by human intelligence in so far as these truths are rooted in the being of the human person and in the constitutive elements of human nature."[8] For May, God's eternal law embraces not only general precepts (that we should love God and our neighbor), but more particular and specific norms that are "absolutely binding, and transcend historical and cultural situations."[9]

While appreciative of certain features of personalism and the natural law tradition, Gustafson has limited confidence in the power of human reason, and in the role of nature to generate a Christian ethics. Rather, he holds that a *religious* ethics is quite different from a philosophical ethics in which human concerns and values hold ultimate importance. Here Gustafson distances himself from those Jewish and Christian ethicists who provide moral insights into health care, sexuality, or modern warfare through either a literal reading of Scripture, or a reasoned reflection on natural phenomena. He stands by his belief that in *religious* ethics normative rules pertaining to human behavior properly flow from grace inspired religious convictions about God, the ultimate reality in whom humans live, move, and have their being. In taking this stand, Gustafson departs from Aristotle, Kant, Mill, Fletcher, Richard McCormick and the majority of Roman Catholics working in social ethics who have prized "unaided" reason's powers, and looked upon human nature as the source of divinely inscribed laws or meanings. In Gustafson's eyes, the "theological qualifies ethics" when agents take serious account of God's nature, purpose, and relations to the world, when theologians creatively integrate these convictions and insights into their theories and decisions about birth control, abortion, the environment, and physician assisted suicide.[10] Humans are God's stewards, according to Gustafson; and stewardship means that we care for ourselves, as individuals, as communities, as institutions, and as a species.

It means that we act in cooperation with and in the service of God's wider ends and purposes.

This rejection of personalism and natural law morality is associated with Gustafson's existential history, and his preference for the reformed tradition. He finds the first's perspective too narrow, too self-serving; the second, flawed, because it exaggerates the intellect's ability to develop normative principles derived from reflection on human nature. On the positive side, Gustafson's "theocentric" moral theory is grounded in a distinctive belief in God's transcendence and in what John Calvin called the *sensus divinitatis*—the recognition of the determinancies and limitations in human life and choice. Happily separating himself from recent trends in Christian social morality nowhere has Gustafson taught that psychological insights into personal wholeness provide *religious* answers to questions about morality or holiness. Rather, while alert to science, and interested in its methods, Gustafson has argued that taking one's convictions about God seriously should lead to changes in one's behavior, because it reorients one's moral point of view.

Gustafson's God: Closer to Calvin than to Aquinas

Gustafson's vision of "God" is not everybody's. He notes that, although the dominant strand of Western ethics has consistently maintained that the material considerations for morality should be derived from purely human reference points (and has focused on the question, What is good for man?), history shows signs of another—and quite different—approach. This can be seen, for instance, in (i) Plato's *Laws*: "Now God ought to be to us the measure of all things, and not man as men commonly say" (88); (ii) in Hindu ethics where "human life is set within a cosmic and natural context in such a way that the cosmic is supreme and that, in a sense, man is made for the cosmos rather than the cosmos for man" (89). Further, Gustafson sees some evidence of this orientation in: (iii) The Bible, specifically in the story of God's command to Abraham to sacrifice Isaac (89); and (iv) in current biology and zoology which provide little support for the dominant Western (pre-Copernican) worldview with its fixation on human interests (90–91).

Kant, like the majority of Christian moralists and Enlightenment philosophers, held that the human person is the measure as well as the measurer of God. However, on the basis of the Biblical and traditional evidence indicated above, Gustafson asks whether "the apparent assumption that man is the moral measure of all things can be sustained" (91). And taking a stand that places him within a small group of Western theologians, he makes this startling conclusion: That there is good reason to doubt that the Deity has designed all created things for the human species as the chief end of his creative work (92). Consequently, the material considerations for a normative ethic are to be derived not only with reference to the human species but also with reference to the place of human beings in a larger ordering of life in the cosmos and in cosmic history (92). Here lies the basis of Gustafson's call that Christian morality becomes all embracing, and long-sighted.

These convictions about religious morality result in conclusions similar to Einstein's views of relativity, and space-time. They turn Christian ethics inside out by displacing the individual and the human species from the center of reality. However, Gustafson does not intend to undermine the "significance" of the human species, a belief that has been protected by Scripture, tradition, the Enlightenment, and romanticism (101–106). He acknowledges problems for individual self-interest and personal autonomy in his turn toward a theocentric ethic (106–108). Nevertheless, he maintains that, "Moral certainty grounded in the will of God, for religious persons, provides the greatest possible authorization for either refraining from or engaging in certain actions and causes" (108). Gustafson remains convinced that the effort to develop an authentic Christian ethic, one more solidly based on what we now know about God's eschatological designs, demands that "man as a species, individuals as persons, and human communities be redescribed in relation to other aspects of nature, to powers beyond their control, to a destiny which is not in human hands, and to a termination which . . . will be without us" (109).

Pope John Paul II's historic encyclical *Veritatis Splendor* (1993) depicts the moral life in terms of God's encounters and human responses; it sees morality in terms of the story of the rich young man in Matthew's gospel: God lovingly invites individuals to "Come, follow me" (Matthew 19:21). This invitation is extended to all who approach Jesus in search of eternal life, who accept Jesus and hold fast to him, and who partake of his life and destiny.[11] There can be little doubt that, although Gustafson's theocentric ethic has some ties to the pope's approach, to preChristian and Christian ethics, it stands quietly apart from the mainstream of Western moral philosophy and religious ethics. Here, God is not a "utilitarian" as Mill believed; the Deity is not the guarantor of human benefits (112), nor is man's salvation the goal of God's creative work (as Athanasius taught). Moreover, if we must rethink the place of the human species in the universe (as Gustafson says we must), then, some moral rules will change in some "uncomfortable" ways for humans (113).

Obviously, Gustafson does not support the approach (defended by Bernard Brady) which describes morality in terms of human flourishing, and with what it means to be a person (both "being" and "doing").[12] His ethics has little in common with Joseph Fletcher's Situation Ethics, with its emphasis on Christ's love, and its act-utilitarian approach to moral decision-making.[13] Gustafson writes: "Human purposes and human conduct have to be evaluated not simply on the basis of considerations derived from reflection about what is good for man. Rather, reflection is needed on how human life is to be related to a moral ordering objective to our species. It may be that the task of ethics is to discern the will of God—a will larger and more comprehensive than an intention for the salvation and well-being of our species, and certainly of individual members of our species" (113). Here is a cosmic vision which Gerard Manley Hopkins would appreciate.[14]

Reason and Religion in Gustafson's Theocentric Ethics

Given its orientation and the inherent difficulty of grasping God's will, Christian discernment will usually not provide any "certain" answers; it will be filled with "risks." With Burton L. Visotzky, author of *The Genesis of Ethics* (1996), Gustafson reminds us that like life, moral dilemmas are often quite messy, that suicide, for example, "is always a tragic moral choice; it is sometimes a misguided choice. But it can be, I believe, a conscientious choice."[15] Indeed, the best Christian decisions will be "tragic" in many circumstances from the human point of view (113). Here, once more, Gustafson turns his back on the Enlightenment's confidence in reason's ability to control nature, and to progress steadily toward an always better future. His writing recalls to our minds the Bible's central warning: *Humanum est errare*.

As Gustafson moves toward applying his theory in the areas of marriage and family, population and nutrition, biomedical research and medical funding, he takes several additional and important methodological stands.[16] First, that in morality and religion there are affective as well as cognitive aspects of experience (119). With W.D. Ross, however, Gustafson maintains that the "good" is not merely inclined toward or felt; it is also known, and thus there is a cognitive aspect as well (119). Second, experiences are "articulated, explained, and given their human meaning through cultures, and cultures are the products of societies and social experiences,"—in other words human experience has a deeply social character (120ff). This implies that: Explanations and meanings, both secular and religious, are socially interpreted and tested (124); they are always framed and limited by the boundaries of the particular communities to which they belong (125). "Righteousness" has a special meaning for Jews, for example, and "justification" has a distinctive meaning for Lutherans. In Gustafson's eyes, his own religious ethic, like all theologies, belongs to a particular tradition (reformed), and it possesses linguistic, religious, and cultural features specific to that tradition's social experiences.[17]

Gustafson is not radically postmodern. He does not hold that Christian morality cannot cross the borders of culture and language. But he does affirm that every moral tradition belongs to language and cultural systems, and that these are vital to the life, growth, and understanding of an ethic. Nevertheless, Gustafson is convinced that religions are historical phenomena that change (just as nations and cultures change), throughout the course of the centuries (136).[18] Consequently, religious leaders must be sensitive to theological or liturgical developments, and to how they restrict the process of cultural adaptation. If they are too strict (as Gustafson thinks Pope John Paul II has been), the leader runs the risk of fragmenting healthy developments. Finally, both revealed religion, and natural theology are grounded in human experience, and are subject, therefore, to its characteristics (149). On the basis of these insights, Gustafson provides a precise statement of his understanding of the role of a Christian ethicist, and of his own personal task: He sees himself as the developer of three central aspects of the Reformed (Calvinist) tradition: (a) The centrality of piety or religious affections (reverence, awe, respect, a sense of responsibility) which is evoked by (b) a sense of a powerful Other, an awareness of God's sovereignty, (c) an understanding of human life as a relationship to the Almighty to whom we are to relate ourselves and all things (157–193). Here Gustafson assists all involved in theology to better understand their social, pastoral, and prophetic roles.[19]

When he looks at how human affections and virtues rise, and become "religious," Gustafson defends a holism now characteristic of feminist ethicists. His remarks about the "religious" significance of "nonreligious" experiences (in nature, history, culture, society, self) stress unity and integration. Gustafson writes: "The religious affections are human *responses*. They are not acts; in the sense that I choose to respond with delight to a landscape or with remorse to suffering I have caused. Nor, as has been indicated, are the affectivities uniquely religious. . . . Often affectivities are responses to particular events, but they can become general dispositions to respond to many events" (229).

There is nothing of Duns Scotus's hairsplitting here; and the same features are evident throughout Gustafson's summary articulation of Western religion's themes about God (as creator, sustainer, governor, judge, redeemer). His comments are built upon the insight that "Respect and awe evoked by nature, history, culture, society, and by our capacities as persons, lead to acknowledgment of the creative powers on which all things depend. God as Creator, remains, in piety, a vivid religious symbol" (238).

Holism, integration, and harmony are essential, as well, to Gustafson's position on the use of scientific data in theology: One cannot draw scientific conclusions or hypotheses from theological statements, and theology cannot explain the world scientifically (257). Further, one cannot draw theological conclusions deductively from scientific data and theories (257). Nevertheless, the sciences do provide some useful support for the religious ethics which Gustafson is developing—the religious sense of dependence upon powers beyond ourselves, for instance, is supported by data and theories from a number of the sciences (260–261). Likewise, physics and biology provide evidence of an order and ordering of natural processes (262–263).[20] On the other hand, some traditional affirmations about God are so incongruous with science, Gustafson believes, that they should now be set aside. For instance, that God has full and total foreknowledge of all historical events (267); God will come to earth to judge the living and the dead (268); God possesses Intellect and Will (270); and God as Person (271). Here scholastic and more conservative theologians will have difficulties with Gustafson.

Theocentric Ethics: A Working Summary

The structure of Gustafson's ethics emerges from the final pages of his two volume work. He states: "We have capacities to discern in particular events and relations something of what the divine governance requires, what our appropriate actions and relations are to nature, to other persons, and so forth. God is the ultimate source of the conditions for the possibilities of all our actions; we do not only respond to these possibilities, but in some instances at least, they respond to us and interact with our action. . . . Our responses to divine governances are always in particular occasions, times, and places" (274). Since Gustafson sees the human as a "valuing" animal, dependent and interdependent, he holds that human life should be construed in continuity with "nature" as much as in distinction from it (282). Also, he maintains that man is a flawed agent, and no single metaphor is sufficient to account for all aspects of the human fault (304). But in order to repair his flaws(as best he can), man needs: (a) To change and enlarge his vision; (b) to change his heart; (c) and to adopt different standards for behavior (308). Gustafson knows that what he is recommending "entails reassessments of many other features of what has been religiously and culturally traditional" (311), and that it will alter some of the traditional moral rules (316).

How do individuals come to reliable conclusions about the morality of modern warfare? How do Christians make safe decisions about abortion or physician-assisted suicide? Gustafson does not leave his readers groping for information about this subject: Discerning what the divine governance enables and requires, and about appropriate relations of ourselves and all things to God, involves research, analysis, and evaluation—reflective, rational activity—about the necessary conditions for life (not necessarily individual or human) to be sustained and developed (339). This enquiry will lead neither to a radical relativism in ethics nor to a denial of absolutes however (340). But the ethics developed by Gustafson does not provide anybody with any absolute moral certainty nor does it eliminate tragedy; it does not guarantee happiness. Rather this approach to making moral judgments, "requires consenting to the governance of the powers of God, and joining in those purposes that can be discerned," Gustafson writes. "God does not exist simply for the service of man; man exists for the service of God" (342). And this is because, as Jonathan Edwards said, "The last end for which God has made moral agents must be the last end for which God has made all things" (342).

Gustafson's Theocentric Ethics: Comment & Critique

When Anglicans are asked to identify the authority by which they make ethical judgments, they usually appeal to three sources: Scripture, tradition, and reason.[21] As readers will have gathered from this synopsis of Gustafson's *magnum opus*, the author takes a creative, independent, and contemporary approach to moral authorities; his ethics solves a number of problems, and creates others. First, unlike John Jefferson Davis, and others who develop evangelical moral theories, Gustafson does not give the Bible a uniquely normative place in his ethics. Rather he holds that God's governance is not revealed to us in its moral details in the Bible, and, further, that the use of the Scriptures to gain insight into God's laws must be in accord with their contributions to theology (339).[22] Like Richard Hooker, Gustafson takes the position that Christians in every age must judge to what extent a passage of Scripture is intended to apply to their own situation, that not all the laws of Scripture are to be understood as binding for all time, and that some are manifestly intended for particular times and places, but not forever.[23] In Gustafson's judgment, Scripture does not stand as an absolute norm of the moral life (a *"norma normans non normata"*), nor does it control Christian theology, liturgy or piety. Rather theology controls Scripture—a position that will be difficult to accept for those who view the Bible as God's absolute and always binding word about right living.[24]

Tradition and reason play important roles in Gustafson's ethics. However, the Reformed tradition provides "theocentric" ethics with shaping methodological insights into religion and morality, not with a large body of prefabricated prescriptive norms or rules. The tradition colors Gustafson's vision of God, and his selection of authors. Thus, Gustafson's analyses of health care and environmental issues concentrate on the service of God, the future, and the wider implications of government and research policies.

When Gustafson speaks about marriage and family, his thought is not determined by icons, ancient synods or patristic tomes (as an Orthodox theologian's might be). His key question is, "What is God enabling and requiring us to be and to do as participants in the patterns and processes of interdependence in marriage and family life?"[25] Gustafson's reasoned and analytical approach to morality, and his desire to make morality rigorous, have their affinities with Anglican morality, and with the Roman Catholic moral tradition. Carefully discerning the physical and cultural patterns and processes is crucial to his theory. It is true that Gustafson says little about the place of intuition in making moral decisions, and nowhere does he dwell upon inner lights or personal revelations. Nor does he write about the role of Holy Spirit, or the moral imagination in communal or personal decision-making. The place of reason can be seen throughout his "theocentric" ethics: Gustafson gives a major task to logic and orderly analysis; he gives a central place to the findings of the natural and physical sciences in making religious moral judgments. Clearly, he is a *20th century* theologian.

Creation plays a central role in Gustafson's theory. However, as already mentioned, Gustafson has consciously distanced himself from "natural law" morality's emphasis on "right reason reflecting on nature." Nature has no absolute authority in his "theocentric" ethics. Where

Catholic moral theology, as seen in Richard A. McCormick's approach, now keeps its eyes fixed on the human "person" as its primary source of data for making decisions about ethical behavior,[26] Gustafson affirms that moral values and principles are backed by, or grounded in, the patterns and processes of interdependence—but these considerations cannot resolve moral questions unless they are related to convictions about what God is calling humans to be and to become, and to transcendent, not purely physical or human considerations, whether individual or national. Where McCormick will be satisfied to settle a moral issue (letting a comatose patient die), in terms of its "benefits and burdens," Gustafson will take the wider perspective. Unlike William E. May, Gustafson does not believe that natural processes provide absolute or immutable laws to which human activity must be conformed.

For this theologian, the natural course of events is not necessarily morally or humanly normative in light of the ends that life and health serve.[27] We are to relate all things in a manner appropriate to their relations to God—but there are no divinely initiated or infallibly revealed prescriptions of proper actions; we cannot know what we should do from reading directly off the patterns of interdependence of life, because there is no moral blueprint in nature.[28] Gustafson gives an important place to experience in developing his approach. Nevertheless, while sympathetic to feminist ethics, his theory does not give a central place to the sources of human experience favored by feminists, such as women's literature, journals, letters, and diaries.[29] Further, Gustafson does not give women's experience a special place in his ethics, nor does his *magnum opus* draw upon the morality one finds in Dante or Shakespeare, George Eliot or G.M. Hopkins, Flannery O'Connor or Walker Percy, Toni Morrison or Adrienne Rich. Indeed, Gustafson's ethics does not say much about the role of cultural narratives in shaping a community's sense of self and the world, a methodological insight central to Roger Betsworth's *Social Ethics: An Examination of American Moral Traditions* (1990). As well, this theory exhibits a somewhat limited view of the role of the liberal arts (painting, poetry, stories, plays), as valuable sources of knowledge for Christians seeking solutions to today's moral problems.

Gustafson's view of the classic moral authorities is summarized in the closing words of his ethics: "The task of ethics is to use knowledge and intelligence to discern, under the inexorable conditions of finitude, how we are to relate ourselves and all things in a manner appropriate to our and their relations to God. It is to seek how to participate in nature and society, in history and culture, and in the ordering of ourselves so that human life is in the service of God, the power that brings all things into being, sustains them and bears down on them, and creates the conditions of possibility for newness and renewal. We are fated never to have the certainty we desire in the human condition."[30] For Gustafson, discerning God's will (active, changing, and contemporary)—not simply assessing individual selfishness or human happiness—is crucial to making correct moral judgments—a theme not easily reconciled with Fletcher's Situationism, or Mills' Utilitarianism where loving one's neighbor is the same as loving God.[31]

The Church, Christ, and the Sovereign God in Gustafson's Ethics

These and other issues were central to a series of essays on Gustafson's ethics published in the *Journal of Religious Ethics* in 1985. Stanley Hauerwas concentrated on "Time and History in Theological Ethics," Lisa Sowle Cahill and Richard McCormick focused on Gustafson's theism, while Paul Ramsey authored a 30 page letter that raised a host of apparent difficulties. Besides these astute observations, there are other methodological problems in Gustafson's ethics: The theory does comment on the place of the faith community in the formation of morality,[32] and recognizes the social aspects of morality. However, Gustafson does not give a unique place to the Christian Church as a moral guide and authoritative teacher. Religious communities shape individual choices and the ethos of cultures, but the morality that these communities foster is "generally not unique, though they may have distinctive religious and theological backings for it."[33] Moreover, *Ethics from a Theocentric Perspective* contains no detailed treatment of the place of the church's historic or current moral teaching in the formation of authentic ethics; it is silent, as well, about such subjects as the respect that should be shown to the pastoral statements of church leaders, synods, or councils.[34] Gustafson believes that "The simpleminded moralism that Protestant churches (more than the Roman Catholic Church) engage in is morally irresponsible. . . ."[35] Here Catholics and Orthodox Christians will find Gustafson's work wanting. Further, in his efforts to unify the religious and nonreligious, Gustafson has weakened some traditional distinctions; and he has reduced the place of "grace" in the moral life. Prayer and the ritual sacraments are scarcely mentioned. Christ-centered theories of Christian ethics have a history that starts in Paul's Epistles, and the Gospels. Gustafson's theory has been criticized for not giving Christ an adequate place in his ethics.[36] Jesus' theocentric piety forms a model for Christians, but it forms simply a part of Christian morality, according to Gustafson.[37] Jesus' cross, and the way of the cross, are revealing symbols of what is enabled and required of persons who seek to serve and glorify God.[38] However, Gustafson does not ground the material norms of his theory on Jesus' life or teaching, nor does he focus his theory on Jesus, the man for others, but on God's sovereignty. Conservative Christians have been shocked by Gustafson's departures from traditional Trinitarian theology. Rather than Aquinas' vision of a gift-giving and beneficent Deity who created all things for human use and benefit, Gustafson prefers a rather different God. While there is biblical support for his position, this understanding of God's nature, creative and saving work, seems somewhat selective and arbitrary.[39]

Conclusion: Calling Christians to Discern God's Patterns of Empowerment

One must applaud Gustafson's thoughtful efforts to link the human species to other life forms, and his patient attempts to refocus Christian morality away from humans. However, it is hard to see exactly how non-human ends and values (other aspects of nature) will be correctly taken into account in developing the rules and principles of Christian moral action. Gustafson does provide us with broad parameters and impressionistic outlines but little more.[40] For example, it is reasonably obvious—simply in human terms—that it is immoral for a community to expend limitless resources on weapons of mass destruction. It is more difficult, however, to make this same judgment if one takes into account the possibility (popular in science fiction) that current human weapons are simply "toys" when compared with those developed millions of years ago by alien species (The Shadows) who will be visiting us some day on missions of conquest! Maybe the WCC's experts and committees are able to grasp some sense of what God is enabling and requiring humans to be and to do, but not individual Christian nurses, teachers, and parents—or the base communities within which these people seek to find life and strength.[41]

There is merit in any ethic which forces humans to look beyond themselves, and to examine the long-term implications of their behavior. Christian morality must be different from secular ethics—as Gustafson emphasizes. Reminding Christians to be "theocentric" rather than self-centered will protect them from lapsing into selfishness and blindness —it will preserve God's intended relationships.

NOTES

[1] Karl Barth, *Church Dogmatics*, III/4 (Edinburgh: T&T Clark, 1961), 351–356.

[2] Emil Brunner, *The Divine Imperative* (London: Lutterworth, 1937), 53–54, 59.

[3] John Howard Yoder, *The Politics of Jesus* (Grand Rapids: Eerdmans, 1972). Two examples of theocentric ethics applied to other areas of life are: Richard A. Young, *Healing The Earth: A Theocentric Perspective on Environmental Problems and Their Solutions* (Nashville: Broadman & Holman, 1994); Stephen H. Webb, *The Gifting God: A Trinitarian Ethics of Excess* (New York: Oxford University Press, 1996).

[4] Pope John Paul II, "Christian Vocation of Spouses May Demand Even Heroism," *L'Osservatore Romano,* October 10, 1983, 7, 16. For a thorough survey of the Pope's thought, Edward Vacek, "John Paul II and Cooperation with God," *The Annual of the Society of Christian Ethics,* edited by Dianne M. Yeager (1990), 81–107.

[5] James M. Gustafson, *Can Ethics Be Christian?* (Chicago: University of Chicago Press, 1975).

[6] Gustafson, *Ethics*, I, 87–113. For a useful list of Gustafson's publications see, "Bibliography of the Writings of James Gustafson, 1951–1984," *Journal of Religious Ethics* (JRE) 13, 1 (Spring 1985), 101–112.

[7] William E. May, "The Vatican Declaration on Sexual Ethics and the Moral Methodology of Vatican Council II," *Linacre Quarterly*, 52, 2 (May 1985), 116–199.

[8] *Ibid.*, 121.

[9] *Ibid.*, 121.

[10] On this aspect of Gustafson's approach, Allen Verhey, "On James M. Gustafson: Can Medical Ethics Be Christian?" In *Theological Voices in Medical Ethics*, edited by Allen Verhey and Stephen E. Lammers (Grand Rapids, MI: Eerdmans, 1993), 30–56, at 31–39.

[11] On this subject, Maura Anne Ryan, "'Then Who Can Be Saved?': Ethics and Ecclesiology in *Veritatis Splendor*," in *Veritatis Splendor: American Responses*, edited by Michael E. Allsopp and John J. O'Keefe (Kansas City: Sheed & Ward, 1995), 1–15, at 2–3.

[12] Bernard V. Brady, *The Moral Bond of Community: Justice and Discourse in Christian Morality* (Washington, DC: Georgetown University Press, 1998), 75–77.

[13] On this subject, Michael E. Allsopp, "Joseph Fletcher's Situation Ethics: 25 Years after the Storm," *Irish Theological Quarterly*, 56, 3 (Summer 1990), 170–190.

[14] On Hopkins's theocentric moral vision, Michael E. Allsopp, "G.M. Hopkins, Narrative, and the Heart of Morality: Exposition & Critique," *Irish Theological Quarterly*, 60, 4 (1994), 287–307.

[15] Ethics, II, 215.

[16] For Gustafson's reflections on environmental ethics see, James M. Gustafson, *A Sense of the Divine: The Natural Environment from a Theocentric Perspective* (Cleveland: Pilgrim Press, 1994).

[17] While some will fear the implications of this point, those who have any knowledge of Irish culture and history will acknowledge its validity and soundness.

[18] The importance of seeing ourselves as historical, social, and cultural persons, and that change takes place in cultures, are central themes in Kevin T. Kelly's *New Directions in*

Sexual Ethics: Moral Theology and the Challenge of AIDS (London: Geoffrey Chapman, 1998), at 27–34.

[19] Kant, as Gustafson notes, saw morality as the basis of religion, and religion as the application of moral laws to the knowledge of God. Gustafson reverses this relationship in his own "Copernican" revolution. On this subject, *Ethics*, II, 116–141, at 138–139.

[20] For a more recent statement on the role of science in theology see, James M. Gustafson, *Intersections: Science, Theology, and Ethics* (Cleveland: Pilgrim Press, 1996).

[21] Earl H. Brill, *The Christian Moral Vision*, The Church Teaching Series, #6 (New York: Seabury Press, 1979), 12.

[22] Obviously, Scripture does not have a formative role in Gustafson's ethics as it does in liberation theology's approaches to morality, and to moral development.

[23] Gustafson, II, 153.

[24] The role of Scripture in Christian ethics has been a subject of major concern in recent years. For an important analysis of the issue, one more conservative than Gustafson's, yet influenced by his writing see, Allen Verhey, *The Great Reversal: Ethics and the New Testament* (Grand Rapids: Eerdmans, 1984). Also, Michael E. Allsopp, "The Role of Sacred Scripture in Richard A. McCormick's Ethics," *Chicago Studies*, 35 (August 1996), 185–196.

[25] *Ethics*, II, 153.

[26] For Gustafson's own analysis of the relationship between his ethics and Aquinas's, see *Ethics*, II, 42–64.

[27] *Ethics*, II, 273.

[28] *Ibid.*, 275. From several conversations with Gustafson, it is clear that he understands McCormick's ethics, and he respects the "Natural Law" approach—but he does not consider either to be "theological."

[29] On this subject, Michael E. Allsopp, "Feminist Ethics at Thirty: A Retrospective," *Explorations* 16, 4 (Summer 1998), 5–28.

[30] *Ethics*, II, 322.

[31] On the relationship between Gustafson's theory and Utilitarianism see, *Ethics*, II, 100–116.

[32] *Ethics*, II, 316–319.

[33] *Ibid.*, 317.

[34] For a somewhat different view of Gustafson's view of the role of the church see, Martin L. Cook, "Reflections on James Gustafson's Theological-Ethical Method," *The Annual of the Society of Christian Ethics*, 17 (1997), 13–17.

[35] *Ethics*, II, 318.

[36] This is central to Richard McCormick's essay, "Gustafson's God: Why? What? Where" (Etc.), *JRE* 13, 1 (Spring 1985), 53–70.

[37] *Ibid.*, 22.

[38] *Ibid.*, 22.

[39] For Gustafson's reply to these criticisms, "A Response to Critics," *JRE* 13, 2, (Fall 1985), 185–209.

[40] This is evident, for instance, when Gustafson deals with biomedical research funding, *Ethics*, II, 253–277.

[41] For remarks about his theory and Utilitarianism, *Ibid.*, 100–116. Also, *Ibid.*, 139–140.

Chapter 6

Liberation Theology/Ethics

During the last 30 years, liberation theology has been a powerful, if controversial, force for social change. Based upon traditional scriptural and doctrinal themes, the approach, for those who support it, is not so much a new way of doing Christian theology and ethics, as a classic model adapted to special contexts. Possessing some of the characteristics found in feminist, situation, and virtue ethics, liberation theology is seen as a way of being and doing in the world that challenges Christians to abandon both capitalist and Marxist idolatries. The approach calls those who wish to follow Jesus, as well as all people of goodwill, to commit themselves to an alternative moral vision, and to a way of living that is Christ-centered, freeing, and focused on building communities of virtue, service, and solidarity.

Latin American Liberation Theology: Origins and Emphases

Before examining liberation theology's strengths and weaknesses, its positive contributions to today's understanding of the Christian life and the role of the Church in the modern world, it will be useful to look first at the history of the approach, to isolate and develop its key themes.

Latin American liberation theology appeared during the 1960s.[1] It has been described by Juan Luis Segundo, one of the pioneers of the movement, as "an irreversible thrust in the Christian process of creating a new consciousness and maturity in our faith."[2] Almost immediately after the start of this movement, other liberation theologies began to be noticed: Black, feminist, environmental, and gay.[3] Like feminists and situationists, each liberation theorist in his or her distinctive way, forms part of a broad grassroots effort toward developing what Karl Rahner called a community oriented "dogmatic morality," that is, a personally meaningful, well integrated and ecclesially constructive spirituality in which one tries, with the help of God's grace and the support of others more gifted in the Spirit (as well as in the knowledge of history, philosophy, sociology, psychology), to speak intelligently about God, to grow in wisdom and virtue, and to discern and implement God's will in one's place and time.

As those know who have been teaching or studying the developments in Christian ethics since World War II, Latin American theologies of liberation embody reactions against traditional views of morality, and aggressive responses to prevailing social situations. According to Ricardo Planas, these theologies have been shaped by a variety of specific forces. One force was a mass-based education program developed in rural Brazil by Paulo Freire in the 1950s, a highly successful initiative that taught adults to read and to take active control of their lives. Another was the spread of "basic ecclesial communities" that began in Brazil in the 1960s, a program in which families gathered to listen to Scripture, share their problems, and work toward practical solutions. A third force was the promise of Vatican II, with its emphasis on respect for persons, evangelization, effectively addressing the concerns of the poor, and building a just and peaceful world in cooperation with all people of goodwill.[4] Marxism was another powerful influence.[5]

Liberation theologies grew out of critiques of the Church's ethics. Some of these criticisms are: That the Church's longstanding stress on individual salvation in the next world represents a distortion of Jesus' message; that the Church does not possess any magical effectiveness where salvation is concerned; and that there are not two separate orders—a supernatural order outside history, and a natural order inside history. On the positive side, liberation theologians have tried to give Christian ethics a solid scriptural and doctrinal basis, and they have made serious efforts to relate the data of religious knowledge to the findings of the social sciences. They have also attempted to be pastorally responsible, as well as sensitive to the Church's call to evangelization and world peace.[6]

Contemporary Christians should applaud Latin American liberation theology's efforts to link salvation and liberation. Like Joseph Fletcher's situation ethics, liberation theology has also emphasized method more than content.[7] According to Segundo, "the one thing that can maintain the liberating character of a theology is not its content but its method" (192). As well, the approach has stressed the importance of renewing Roman Catholic theology, and it has emphasized the need for an ethics more authentically Christian, scientific, and practical.

With Bernard Haring, Joseph Fuchs, Hans Urs von Balthasar, Edouard Hamel, John Giles Milhaven, Lisa Sowle Cahill, Margaret Farley, James Gaffney, Enda McDonagh, Charles Curran, Norbert

Rigali, Daniel Maguire, Germain Grisez, and Richard McCormick, the pioneers of liberation theology were justified (I believe) in seeing that Roman Catholic moral theology, as taught in the Church's seminaries during the first part of this century, was seriously defective, because it was self-consciously autonomous (separated from both past and present), discursive (talked about theology rather than encouraged doing theology), static, individualistic, and academic. As a result, they have encouraged major changes based upon their own experiences in Latin America, and their education in psychology, sociology, philosophy, economics, and political science. From the start liberation theology's central question has been, "Since theology is talk about God, how does an intelligent Christian living today speak about God?"[8]

Praxis: Its Essential Place in Liberation Ethics

It is easy to forget the reform recommendations made by these theologians. The most important is based on the conviction that effective theology (reflection, critical attitude) begins with and results from *praxis* rather than creed or catechism. For Gustavo Gutierrez, on whom this chapter will later focus, this methodological starting point builds on the premise that "Only if we start in the realm of practice will we be able to develop a discourse about God that is authentic and respectful."[9] The principle is grounded in an insight basic to monastic pedagogy: First live the Christian life, then reflect; first develop a lifestyle, then speak about God.

This approach insists on the active integration of thought and action (the mutual interaction of theory and practice)—because, in its eyes, to be engaged in theology does not mean to seek an exact, library known familiarity with the writings of Aquinas, Luther or Calvin, but to be involved in ministry and engaged in the critical interpretation of history in the light of divine revelation. Or, as Berryman says, liberation is both prior to pastoral work and the outgrowth of pastoral work. It is both theory *for* praxis and theory *of* praxis (82).

Praxis, one of the distinctive terms in liberation theology, has generated a variety of meanings, given its place over the centuries in the writings of Aristotle, Hegel, Marx, and Freire. Basically, it means 'practice' and 'experience.' According to Thomas Schubeck, it extends to what sociologist Alfred Schutz calls the world of everyday life, the practical day-to-day coping of people whose decisions are guided by the maxims of a common wisdom.[10] *Praxis* implies life history rather than book knowledge; it means active living rather than armchair analysis;

committed action rather than distanced observation; concrete, hands on involvement rather than objective, impartial speculation. While not all *praxis* has the same truth value, and some cannot be called Christian, for liberation theologians, *praxis* provides a lens through which one is better able to understand issues, and a people's collective or an individual's personal *praxis* constitute foundational sources of religious and ethical insight.

The importance of *praxis* in doing theology or making moral decisions is highlighted in the following words taken from Gutierrez's *A Theology of Liberation: History, Politics and Salvation* (1973). The proclamation of the Gospel has a politicizing function, Gutierrez admits. Consciences are moved whenever people hear Jesus' parables. However, the Gospel proclamation becomes real and meaningful only when it is lived and announced "from within a commitment to liberation, that is, only in concrete, effective solidarity with people and exploited social classes. It is not by academic study, but, by participating in a community's struggles can we understand the implications of the Gospel message and make it have an impact on history" (83).

Segundo reinforces these words: "*We* can only have an authentic faith and do theology in a genuine way when we have committed ourselves to an authentic struggle that opens our eyes to the new possibilities and meaning of God's word" (97). It is *praxis* that makes progressive Latin American theology more interested in *being liberative* rather than in *talking about liberation* (9).

Gutierrez has highlighted other significant features of this reality.[11] In his view, Christian *praxis* means contemplative prayer (silence), and religious commitment within history (action). Further, *praxis* teaches that genuine theology (speaking about God) can be undertaken only by freely following in the footsteps of Jesus, the liberator or messiah of the poor, who led his disciples to the God of the Exodus, and taught an ethics of service and self-sacrifice (549). *Praxis* shows, as well, that everything has a political color; that religious and social relationships fall within political spheres; that an authentic Christian ethics must be a political ethics; and therefore, that the church's work must involve more than saving 'souls' and worshiping God. Moreover, when theology is done in Latin America, *praxis* necessitates that the problems of the poor and the oppressed are primary concerns, indeed, that theology must embody an option for the poor (549).[12]

For these reasons, *praxis* (for liberation theologians) is essential to any sound theology. It is its "first step." Thus, theology becomes, "a critical reflection, in the light of the Divine Word received in faith, on the presence of Christians in the world" (549). Such a *praxis*-centered theology makes the values of faith, hope, and charity explicit. It necessitates that moral decisions be worked out not in advance, or outside of the actual historical process but only within the process —which in the Latin-American context means that Christian ethics is a "ethics of liberation," a morality that commits itself to the poor, and to building humane and just societies.

Theology will have somewhat different responses to its controlling question when done on other continents such as Africa, Asia, Europe, and Australia. However, in Gutierrez's judgment, theology's central question in Latin America today is, "How are we to speak of God in the face of the poverty, ignorance, suffering, disease and death of the innocent?" (550).

Liberation Theology & Academic Theology: Worlds Apart

Besides the differences already mentioned, liberation theologians have pointed out some other fundamental differences between their theology and traditional academic theology. They feel compelled (rightly, I believe) to combine the disciplines that open up the past with those sciences that best help to explain the present (8). Consequently, liberation theologians have used both classic sciences (history and exegesis) as well as modern sciences, in their renewal efforts. They have actively employed the social sciences, sociology, psychology, and economics, in their attempts to better understand such subjects as political power, the institutional causes of poverty and oppression, the influence of "ideologies," and the unconscious social factors that have influenced the formulation of the church's ecclesiology, eschatology, canon law, and moral theology. Liberation theologians understand the place of myths and narratives in shaping social consciousness (56).

For Segundo, Gutierrez and Leonardo Boff, the social sciences are not pretheological or nontheological disciplines; they avoid such dualisms, arguing that these fields contribute constitutively to their theological methods. Without these scientific tools, they would not be able to properly grasp the economic or political dimensions of reality, and thereby accurately understand the Christian faith in *praxis*.

Liberation Theology's Hermeneutical Circle

As one looks back on the 20th century, its wars, and its famines, one must admire Segundo and other liberation theologians for their bold criticism of Catholic theology for largely evading the century's contemporary problems, and for not addressing the great issues in biology, health, evolution and social change (116). One should also admire how they have used sociological tools to assist in developing methods of dealing with past and present—especially in relating the teaching of Scripture with modern problems through a process they call the *hermeneutic circle*—the constant change in our interpretation of the Bible which is dictated by the continuing changes in our present-day reality, both individual and societal. "Hermeneutic" means "having to do with interpretation." And the circular nature of this interpretation occurs because each new reality obliges us to interpret the word of God afresh, to change reality accordingly, and then to go back and reinterpret the word of God again, and so on (8).

Segundo, Boff, and Gutierrez have forced the church to take a stand about their firm belief that God addresses us today as God addressed the Hebrews in the days of Moses: *Within concrete events*. They have raised the consciousness of Christians by emphasizing that God's word is incarnated in contemporary history as it was in the history of the first Christians. In other words, liberation theology and ethics have shaped today's faith by maintaining that God communicates in historical moments; that the Bible contains living normative records of these communications within cultural and religious narratives (Genesis story, fall story, Exodus story), and that, as we read these stories today, they interactively shape and mold, explain, and define both past and present divine communications.

The Exodus story provides a prime example of this approach to Scripture.[13] The story was read by the Hebrew people during the time of the Babylonian exile, and used by them to give meaning to their lives. The same story was read later by the first Christian communities, and the narrative provided them with inspiration and understanding about Jesus, his death and resurrection. It was read later still by European and American communities (Baptists), and provided them with insights into God's dealings in their lives and conditions. Unlike Roman Catholic moral theologians' teaching prior to World War II, who made no reference to this event, liberation theologians argue that the story of the Exodus, when contemplated today by committed Christians living in Latin America, Africa, and Asia, sheds light upon their efforts to respond to God's will in this time—to see how the living God sides with the oppressed against the Pharaohs (the rich, the elite, and the military) of this world.[14]

This is the circular method by which we should read Scripture, the highest authority and last word in theology—from *praxis* to Bible, from

Bible to *praxis*. And in this dynamic learning process we find new insights and solutions; in the process we become different, as we more fully grasp meanings and solutions locked in God's word. "People engaged in a *praxis* confer added meaning to the text, and a faithful reading of the text gives new meaning and direction to their *praxis*," Schubeck writes. "As Gutierrez is fond of saying, we read Scripture—seen as 'the book of life'—from within the context of our own *praxis*, but Scripture also reads us by effecting change in us" (131). Who can deny that this contemplative reflection on Scripture was the way that Jesus, Augustine, and Ignatius Loyola came to discern the signs of the times?

The Use of Scripture in Liberation Ethics: The Basis for *Praxis*

When one examines how the Bible was used in the Roman Catholic manuals of moral theology, one quickly sees that Latin American liberation theology provides a distinctive and largely forgotten way of using Scripture in ethics. However, unlike evangelical ethicists, liberation theologians such as Gutierrez, Segundo, and Jon Sobrino, do not use the Bible's moral commands or its implications as immediate answers for today's issues. They do not cite statements or commands as sources for concrete answers to today's questions about capital punishment or physician-assisted suicide. Rather they focus on developing a liberating spirituality based in Scripture's narratives and supported by the Christian faith (its doctrines of incarnation, grace, freedom, and human dignity). They seek the growth of a vision and value system that would challenge Christians to commit themselves to the reign of God. Liberation ethicists are spiritual directors more than moralists; they have concentrated on guiding the commitment and freedom of moral decision-makers, not on articulating norms directly tied to the Bible for making today's ethical decisions.

From the start, liberation ethics was a morality that emphasized coming to know and work with God and Jesus Christ in relation to one's neighbors—especially the widowed, poor, and orphaned in one's community. In Alfred Hennelly's estimate, liberation morality is *creative*, and *progressive*; it is not an ethics of the licit and illicit, but one suitable for the construction of love.[15] It is essentially *social*, and *significative* (it is a sign, and light in the world). Liberation ethics is different from the lived morality we find in the mainstream European or North American church (95).

As we will see in more detail later in this chapter, this ethical model has its obvious strengths. It is Scriptural; it is clear, consistent, and coherent. "Sobrino presents a remarkably consistent vision of the foundation of Christian morality developed from the kingdom of God," Schubeck maintains. "He demonstrates how the imperative (e.g., commit oneself to the poor) arises from a graced encounter with the spirit of Jesus mediated through the Bible, community worship, historical events, and through the poor themselves. His grounding obligation in gratuity respects God's initiative and power, as well as human freedom" (197). The approach avoids some of the problems in evangelical ethics' literalistic use of Scripture, yet at the same time it is more conservative than Sharon Welch's feminist ethics, although, like the latter, it strives boldly to allow for the influence of culture and history, while it tries to incorporate the compelling insights of developmental psychology, and the findings of research into adult spirituality.

Liberation theology has learned important lessons from the social sciences. While it has been criticized from its inception for its use of Marxist categories, it has used both Marxist and postmodern approaches to analyze and interpret Scripture, and to critique society. Modern sociologists have taught these theologians that although 'faith' is an absolute, 'theology' (at its best) is always incomplete, its conclusions never able to be universalized. Its concrete doctrines and principles are always relative—because a person's theology (Paul's, Augustine's, Luther's, Tillich's, Welch's, Gustafson's) can never be totally separated from his or her *ideology*—a concrete thought and value system conditioned by history.[16] Consequently, in Segundo's judgment, even with the Christian faith, each of us lives in the midst of relativism; Christian conduct, like non-Christian conduct, is always subject to a 'human' dose of relativism (175). This does not mean that we live in chaos, however (167), the Church's faith has been incarnated throughout the centuries in successive ideologies, and while it is impossible to wring out 'faith' in its essence—to reduce Christianity to a book or a page of the Bible—it is possible to see in all these successive faith-incarnated ideologies *the road to be traveled* by modern and future Christians (181).

An Alternative Third World Moral Theology of Liberation: Two Summaries

Two expositions of Latin American liberation theology are illuminating. Christine Gudorf has called *Moral Theology: Dead Ends and*

Alternatives a "powerful attempt to do moral theology from a liberation theology perspective." Written by Antonio Moser and Bernardino Leers, two Roman Catholic theologians working in Brazil, the book is a three part study that delineates an ethics that tries to avoid the immorality, permissiveness and amorality the authors find in contemporary academic and Catholic seminary moral theology (2). Employing a summary style that suggests rather than spells out (5) a language system that enables moral theology to be accepted as part of the "good news" proclaimed by Christ (5), Moser and Leers set out to attract rather than to threaten, to bring both an ancient and a new heritage up to date (5). The authors build upon the Scriptural themes of "covenant' (the revelation of God's purpose), and "Kingdom of God" (the heart of Christ's life and message), in order to present a "liberative" ethic that avoids the "no exits" they find in current Catholic ethics (manualistic and renewed).

This short book provides (its authors believe) "the essential services to make the building [of Christian morality] work" by "re-cladding" it in ways that make it more welcoming—because, "It is, after all, in the moral theology building that Jesus' brothers and sisters seek shelter, hoping to feel at home in the Father's house" (3).

Building Stronger Roman Catholic Ethics: Features

The authors are specific about the defects in academic and mainstream Catholic ethics. First, they maintain that the neoscholastic manuals of moral theology used in Roman Catholic seminaries from the 18th century until the 1950s contain a theology basically attuned to the colonial enterprise, and the bourgeois liberal ethos of the times (20). According to Moser and Leers, these widely influential textbooks possessed some worthwhile values (they sought the universal, the perennial, and taught the importance of the individual and law). But they also embodied questionable aspects: They were filled with uncritical certitudes (22), with pessimism and mistrust about humanity, especially with regard to sexuality (23); they were legalistic (23–4); and dominated by a privatistic ethos—a morality excessively concerned with saving individual souls (24–5). Therefore, this way of doing ethics cannot be supported any longer.

The authors maintain that the "renewed" Roman Catholic morality following Vatican II has come a long way in a short time (43). The movement (seen in the work of Richard McCormick, Edouard Hamel, Charles Curran, Enda McDonagh, Margaret Farley, Norbert Rigali, Joseph Fuchs, and Lisa Sowle Cahill) represents an astonishingly fertile current (30) that is more scriptural (36–37), more Christ-centered (37–38), more optimistic, and more socially oriented (38–40). It does contain a definite emphasis on grace (40–41) and love (41–42). However, this approach (in spite of these new strengths) still has serious defects: It is primarily applicable to the First World, and deals mainly with the problems of people who enjoy privileged economic, social, and religious status (45). It is an idealistic rather than a realistic ethics (47–48); it is personalistic rather than social (48); and it is more concerned with reform than with renewal (48–49). For Moser and Leers, "The renewed approach . . . valued historicity, produced a realistic optimism, brought out the power of grace and the release of love" (49). Nevertheless, it is not really a viable alternative for those facing either mass starvation or gross exploitation in Latin America (44).

The alternative ethics that the authors propose did not create its methodology *ex nihilo*, however. Since liberation theology, as we have already seen, considers itself a new way of understanding and doing theology (fashioning a reading of God's word that proceeds from a particular context), it is not surprising that it should insist (in part) on the originality of its methodology, as well as on some other distinctive characteristics (55). These are: To see rather than to judge; to adopt the perspective of the poor; to take social conflictivity seriously, that is, to question, combat, and advocate change; to emphasize *praxis*, and the socio-political dimensions of reality, God, church, persons, and theology (55–59).

The liberation ethics of Moser and Leers seeks to broaden the horizon of Catholic ethics, and to build a new society by integrating the marginalized into the Church. This is done in such a way that they become the protagonists of new insights more in accordance with God's plans (60). This means redressing the balance, and bringing the concerns of the impoverished to the fore (61). Rather than teaching passive acceptance of economic hardships as God's will, liberation ethics teaches legal and land reforms. Besides focusing on the break-down of the family, drugs and alcoholism, such an ethics gives attention to hunger, disease, lack of education, and the effort to put a roof over one's head (61–63)—issues not central to either the seminary manuals or the renewed Roman Catholic ethics.

Gustavo Gutierrez's *The God of Life* (1991), is another three part work that provides a classic example of liberation ethics.[17] The book's Introduction (xi–xviii) provides its readers with a summary of all that will follow. Part I focuses on Scripture to show that "God is love" (I John 4:8)—which means that God liberates because God is the God of life (3). It uses both the Old Testament and the New Testament to illustrate that the "God of Israel makes justice and judgment the foundations of the divine reign, as we find in Psalm 89:15" (20). This means that God is the "*go'el* of the poor among the people" (24), and of the poor of all the people of the earth, a theme central to II Isaiah (24–25). Third, Gutierrez argues that God is near to us and faithful (33–47), and that we must constantly struggle against idolatry and death (48–64). Weaving together themes from the Psalms (52:9; 62:6–7,9,11), Job (22:23–27), Jeremiah (9:22–23), Matthew (21:33–43), and Ezekiel (37:1–14), the author concludes, "In Latin America today the church is bringing into play the sense of its own identity as the community of disciples of him who came that we might 'have life and have it more abundantly' (John 10:10)" (63).

God's Love, God's Presence and Christian Discipleship Today

In the second part of this book, Gutierrez takes up the classic question, "Where is God?" He also answers in the following themes: "The God of the Bible is the God who comes to the people" (69); and "This is the Time of Fulfillment" (98–103). Here the author argues that "The underemployed, the poor, the blind, the crippled, public sinners, Ayacuchan Indians, landless peasants, populations looking for shelter: These are the least members of history. Therefore they are the first objects of the tender love of the God of Jesus Christ. The justice of God is deep and true because it is steeped in gratuitousness. It is this justice that demands an authentic justice of us today" (117).

In providing a summary outline of Christian ethics, Gutierrez does not start with natural law or Aristotle—he states, "The beatitudes in Matthew are . . . the Magna Carta of the congregation (the church) that is made up on the disciples of Jesus" (118). Therefore, it follows that, "Those who build this peace—which implies being attuned to God and God's will in history, as well as a wholeness of life, both personal (health) and social (justice)—will be called 'children of God'; this means that they will *be* children of God" (127). Taking up one of the still divisive issues that separates Protestants and Catholics, the author uses Scripture to show that Christ's disciples are called upon not to be saved by works, but to bear witness to God through concrete actions (131). "Disciples are those who practice justice or righteousness through life giving works of love and thereby glorify the Father," he argues (131). Although Matthew and Luke appear to be quite different, they are (in Gutierrez's view) complementary. "The life of disciples runs its course between gratuitousness and demand, investiture as witness and mission. In his version of the Beatitudes Matthew emphasizes the need of behavior oriented to others. This is a requirement that flows from the gift of the kingdom. Likewise nothing makes greater demands for solidarity with others than the gratuitousness of God's love" (132).

The final part of this book looks at the question, "How are we to talk of God?" Gutierrez's answer comes as no surprise given what has been stated earlier about liberation theology: ". . . talk about God presupposes practice, that is, the silence of contemplation and commitment" (145). Using Job as his guide, the author shows that all who seek to speak about God under the influence of the Spirit, must come to see from experience that God has a special love for the disinherited, that God is not simply the guardian of a rigid moral order, and that no human work, no matter its value, merits grace (162–163).[18] Gutierrez uses Mary ("the perfect Christian"), and Jesus ("the Way, Truth, and Life") to illustrate how contemporary Christian theology should speak about discipleship, and about God's view of women (165–186). This is an important theme, given the fact that women do not enjoy high esteem in some Latin cultures, in spite of centuries of Christian influence.[19]

Liberation Theology: Protestant and Catholic Concerns

Early in the 1970s, the Permanent Council of the French Catholic Bishops said that "Christians would be unfaithful to their mission of evangelizing if they did not mobilize effectively to work with all their brothers, believers and nonbelievers, for human liberation, of each person and all persons."[20] However, Liberation Theology has had many critics throughout its history. Andrew Greeley was one of the early critics.[21] More recently, the American Protestant theologian, Don S. Browning, has written in support of Luis Segundo's concept of the "hermeneutic circle," as described in The Liberation of Theology (1976). He has expressed sympathy for Segundo's "partiality for the poor" as part of the central message of the Christian faith. Browning believes, nevertheless, that Segundo is "so attached to this prejudice, which is doubtless born of his experiences with the struggle of Latin American poor, that he is insensitive to aspects of the Scriptures that this precommitment does not grasp."[22]

On the other hand, the Irish Catholic writer, Vincent MacNamara, praises liberation theology and ethics for giving a fresh and powerful impetus to the well attested biblical theme that faith works through love. "It has also helped to highlight several related themes," MacNamara notes. "That salvation is not just personal and spiritual but social and institutional; that bringing about liberation from oppressive situations is bringing about God's kingdom; that in the Christian tradition God is father of the poor." At the same time, MacNamara questions liberation theology's ability to provide answers to today's complex medical, environmental, and economic issues. "But does it enable the Christian to know what to do: Does it, through its interpretation of revelation, give a specific and concrete insight into what is morally required, what God is requiring and enabling us to do?"[23]

Another contemporary theologian who has positively embraced the central features of liberation theology is Karen Lebacqz. In her *Justice in an Unjust World* (Minneapolis: Augsburg Press, 1987), Lebacqz agrees that a new hermeneutic is needed. "The starting point both for theology and for exegesis and textual interpretation is the lived experience of those who struggle against oceans of injustice," she writes (60). Like Gutierrez and Boff, Lebacqz emphasizes that "the goal of biblical remembrance is not understanding of the text but a new and liberating praxis" (60). She sees the poor as the privileged interpreters of the biblical message, and she grants them a special role in defining God's word. With other liberation theologians, she holds that if a person wants to understand reality as biblical revelation discloses it, then he/she must enter into the interpretational viewpoint of those most needing to be liberated.

At the same time, Lebacqz is fully aware that the Bible embodies limitations, such as a tolerance of slavery and support for the second-class status of women. She is also aware that God is greater than any theory of justice; that God brings about justice to the poor in ways that we cannot imagine in our theories.

Michael Novak's Central Question: Will It Liberate?

Leaving aside the Vatican's concerns about liberation theology, and Pope John Paul II's opposition, one of the best known contemporary American critics of this approach in Christian ethics is Michael Novak, author of *The Spirit of Democratic Capitalism* (1982), "The Quintessential Liberal: John Stuart Mill," in *Freedom with Justice: Catholic Social Thought and Liberal Institutions* (1984), "Democracy and Human Rights," in *Speaking to the Third World: Essays on Democracy and Development*, edited by Peter Berger and Michael Novak (1985), and *Will It Liberate? Questions About Liberation Theology* (1986). There is much in Latin American liberation theology to admire, most of all its intellectual ambition, Novak admits (2). Theologians should take liberation theology seriously. It asks the right questions. It has good intentions (33). "There can be no question that great revolutions in political economy are necessary in Latin America, if that great and much blessed continent is to fulfill its full human destiny," Novak writes (2).

However, Novak is critical of Latin American liberation theology's basic concepts. He disagrees with its image of history, and with its sense that the basic law of creation is oppression (108–110). It is abstract, vague, and general (113). He is most critical of its judgment upon economic activism, commerce, invention, discovery, entrepreneurship, enterprise, investment—in a word, capitalism (3). "Latin American humanism has been hostile to commerce and to economic dynamism, which it considers vulgar, low, of little esteem, and more than a little tainted with evil. Latin American humanism prefers the mode of the aristocratic spirit on the one side, and the simplicity of the rural peasant, on the other. Its basic enlivening vision is feudal. . . ."(3).

Latin America needs a revolution, but it does not need a socialist revolution. This is the central thesis of Novak's book. Latin America needs to throw off its protections for the rich, and strip them of their ancient privileges. It needs to move from being precapitalist to capitalist (5). "It is my hypothesis that the liberal society, built around a capitalist society that promises discovery and entrepreneurship among the poor at the base of society, will succeed more quickly, more thoroughly, and in a more liberating fashion, than the socialist societies so far conceived of by liberation theologians," Novak writes. (8–9). Or as he says later, "Nothing so lifts up the poor as the liberation of their own creative economic activities" (217).

Segundo's Liberation theology is utopian (33). Novak prefers the "liberal" views of those who inspired and built the United States: Adam Smith, John Stuart Mill, Edmund Burke, and Alexis de Tocqueville (35). In place of societies based upon Marxist ideals and economics, Novak argues for a state built upon "democratic capitalism" (38). Liberation theology is too quick to reject capitalism. It is too suspicious of liberalism, capitalism, and modernity (142). When it speaks about "the poor," it speaks solely in terms of "class" and in doing so it does violence to the individuality of each human person (152). When liberation theology talks about "socialism," it fails to respect natural inequalities rooted in individual wills (188).

Novak argues that Latin America will develop much quicker under leaders committed to economic, political, civil, religious and cultural liberties, because "Economic liberties give material substance to political and civil liberties, and to intellectual and artistic liberties. To own printing presses—in general, to have autonomy over economic instruments—is an indispensable condition for other liberties, among incarnate creatures such as we" (217). He supports Latin American liberals who believe in an economy in which ordinary people will be free to choose and to act and to create—without being controlled by "statism" or dominated by socialist secret police (254).

The following provides an insight into Novak's highly theological and ethical position that shows a debt to the Bible, and the natural law tradition. "To be a citizen in a modern society is to bear a new moral destiny. Yet such a destiny is at one with the destiny established for us in the book of Genesis, in which we read that men and women were made in the image of God, the Creator of the Latin American continent, the Creator of all things, the Creator of us all. It is a good creation. Our vocation as Christians and Jews is to seize the clues left by our Creator, in order to bring his work to the beauty he has hidden within it. Our vocation is to do so free from tyranny and free from poverty. Our vocation is to do so both in liberation and in that humane creativity which is the goal of any genuine liberation" (95).

Latin American Liberation Theology: Moving Communities toward Freedom

Like the feminist approach in Christian ethics, liberation theology now takes many different forms. As some Latin American nations have experienced democracy, while others have tasted years of socialism, its proponents have rethought some of their central beliefs regarding religious, political and cultural freedom. The Vatican's concern about liberation theology's Marxism, and Pope John Paul II's open rejection of the approach, have both brought about other changes as well.[24]

During the coming century, the next generation of liberation theologians will have to argue in favor of biblically rich and economically sound approaches that develop and protect what Novak calls "the three fundamental liberations: Freedom in the political order, freedom from poverty, and freedom of conscience, information, and ideas" (228). However, since European and American Protestant and Catholic leaders seem to be critical of liberalism, these writers and pastors will be facing uphill tasks as they develop ethical theories that delineate and protect those inalienable rights endowed in each person by the Creator.

No doubt, some will be inspired in their efforts, not only by the pressing global needs in Third World countries, in particular, those being devastated by AIDS, debt, and genocidal wars, but also by Thomas Jefferson's words, "The God who gave us life gave us liberty." Liberation theology and ethics forces Christian ethics back to its biblical roots; it makes morality a part of daily life. The approach emphasizes a theme omitted by moral theories that focus on the status quo. Because liberation ethics actively integrates morality and spirituality, and has a socially advancing goal, it will always have strong appeal to those who see Christ's message in terms of overcoming the chains of social and personal sin. Because of its inherent simplicity, it will always appeal.

NOTES

[1] On the beginnings of this movement see, Phillip Berryman. *Liberation Theology* (Philadelphia, PA: Temple University Press, 1987), 9–28.

[2] Juan Luis Segundo, *The Liberation of Theology* (Maryknoll, NY: Orbis Books, 1976), 3.

[3] For example, James Cone, *A Black Theology of Liberation* (New York: Lippincott, 1970).

[4] On the role of Vatican II in the origins of liberation theology see, Leonardo Boff, *When Theology Listens to the Poor* (San Francisco, CA: Harper & Row, 1988), 1–31.

[5] Ricardo Planas, *Liberation Theology: The Political Expression of Religion* (Kansas City: Sheed & Ward, 1986), 3.

[6] From liberation theology's emphasis on "seeing, judging, acting," one also sees signs of the influence of the highly successful Catholic youth movement founded by a Belgium priest, Msgr. Joseph Cardijn, called the Young Catholic Worker (YCW) movement. This was a worldwide force for religious education and social action during the 1950s–1960s.

[7] For a summary of the central features of the approach see, Charles E. Curran, "Absolute Moral Norms," in *Christian Ethics: An Introduction*, Bernard Hoose (ed.), (London: Cassell, 1998), 82.

[8] For a useful, if early, bibliography see, Francis P. Fiorenza, "Latin American Liberation Theology," in *Interpretation,* 28 (1974), 441–457.

[9] Gustavo Gutierrez, "Liberation Theology," in *New Dictionary of Catholic Social Thought*, 548–553, at 549.

[10] Thomas L. Schubeck, *Liberation Ethics: Sources, Models, and Norms* (Minneapolis, MN: Fortress Press, 1993), 39. Also, Berryman, 85–87.

[11] Gustavo Gutierrez, "Liberation Theology," *New Dictionary of Catholic Social Thought*, 548–553.

[12] For further on this aspect of liberation theology see, Donal Door, "Poor, Preferential Option for the Poor,' in *New Dictionary of Catholic Social Thought*, 755–759.

[13] On the place of the Exodus in liberation theology see, Norman Lohfink, *Option for the Poor: The Basic Principle of Liberation Theology in the Light of the Bible* (Berkeley: Bibal Press, 1987).

[14] On liberation theology's key Scriptural themes see, Leonardo Boff and Clodovis Boff. *Introducing Liberation Theology* (Maryknoll, NY: Orbis Books, 1987), 43–65.

[15] Alfred T. Hennelly, *Theologies in Conflict: The Challenge of Juan Luis Segundo* (Maryknoll, NY: Orbis Books, 1979), 93–94.

[16] An ideology is "any conception that offers a view of the various aspects of life from the standpoint of a specific group in society." On this subject see, Berryman, 131–134; Planas, 77–125.

[17] Gustavo Gutierrez, *The God of Life*, translated from the Spanish by Matthew J. O'Connell (Orbis Books, New York, 1991).

[18] For further information on this subject, Gustavo Gutierrez, *On Job: God-Talk and the Suffering of the Innocent*, translated by Marvin J. O'Connell (New York: Orbis Books, 1987).

[19] For an important study of Mary in the context of liberation theology see, Ivonne Gebara and Maria Bingemer, *Mary: Mother of God, Mother of the Poor* (New York: Orbis Books, 1989).

[20] For these words, Richard A. McCormick, *Notes on Moral Theology: 1965–1980* (Washington, DC: University Press of America, 1981), 619.

[21] Andrew Greeley, "Theology without Freedom?" *Catholic Chronicle* (November 28, 1975), 5.

[22] Don S. Browning, *A Fundamental Practical Theology: Descriptive and Strategic Proposals* (Minneapolis: Fortress Press, 1991), 66.

[23] Vincent MacNamara, *Faith & Ethics: Recent Roman Catholicism* (Dublin: Gill and MacMillan, 1985), 138.

[24] For a valuable analysis of the Vatican's second instruction on liberation theology see, "Christian Freedom and Liberation" (April 5, 1986), Novak, *op. cit.*, 218–229.

EPILOGUE

The future is prepared in the waiting when the seed, once deposited, puts forth a shoot and grows. What is essential is to have sown the seed. . . . There is a plan of Providence, a general conduct of things, and in this plan, each exists in solidarity with others, and must know how to await the hour that God has fixed.

Yves Congar, O.P.

The changes that have taken place over the last 30 years in Protestant and Roman Catholic "foundational" ethics have been far-reaching. As the six models examined in this book illustrate, there has been a renewed interest in the Bible among Roman Catholics. Due to the worldwide influence of Bernard Haring's *The Law of Christ,* and more recent biblical works, Catholic writers have placed less emphasis on reason and natural law; they have endeavored to develop biblical moralities. At the same time, Church (canon) law, which was central to the manuals of moral theology used in Roman Catholic seminaries until the 1960s, has almost disappeared. Due to the influence of dogmatic theologians, such as Karl Rahner, Paul Tillich, Karl Barth, Yves Congar, and Hans Urs von Balthasar, other major changes have also taken place. Roman Catholic moral theology has become less legalistic and more personalistic, more visibly aware of the dynamic role of the Spirit in history, and of the Christian life as sacramental and grace-filled.

At the same time, as Edward LeRoy Long shows in his monumental surveys of Christian ethics, Protestant writers throughout these years have become more sensitive to Christ's ethical example and less sensitive to Mosaic Law; they have become less insistent on the claims of conscience and more willing to acknowledge the significance of the church's tradition. Like their Catholic colleagues, Protestant theologians have come to see that while morality has its ties to faith and religion, it is also a "science" as Aquinas taught.

Clearly, contemporary Protestant and Catholic moral theories reflect the influences of Joseph Fletcher, Paul Ramsey, Dietrich Bonhoeffer, James Gustafson, Gustavo Gutierrez, and Stanley Hauerwas. They are marked with the signs of post-World War II debates about rules and norms, works and gifts, commands and stories, codes and decisions. Both have been shaped by shared concerns about the poor, women's rights, human development, and the environment.

* * * *

Both the choice and critique of "models," whether in theology or psychology depends, or should depend, on established and shared criteria, as Avery Dulles says in his *Models of the Church* (1974). However, all criteria are tied to values, and as James Gustafson admits, a person's values are associated with life's friendships, experiences, and faith journeys. However, Dulles puts forward seven criteria that he considers useful in assessing the "truthfulness" of models that might be used in dogmatic or moral theology:

- **Basis in Scripture.** This is a central feature of any Christian ethical approach, and the more explicit the model's biblical foundations the more support it will generate.
- **Basis in Tradition.** Not all theologians have the same regard for tradition. It is less important for Gustafson than for John Jefferson Davis, less central to Joseph Fletcher's ethics than to Richard McCormick's.
- **Capacity to give Christians a sense of their corporate identity and mission.** Moral theories do not simply assist individuals to make life or professional decisions. They develop identity and purpose, as well as a sense of mission and discipleship.
- **Tendency to foster the virtues and values generally admired by Christians.** Christians, by definition, are people who follow Christ. They are called to lives of faith, hope, love, honesty, humility, compassion, and forgiveness. A moral model that fosters these values and virtues will have strong support within the Christian Church, whereas one that negates them will not thrive.
- **Correspondence with the religious experience of people today.** Christians today are not facing the problems of medieval communities. They are living with AIDS, bio-terrorism, and weapons of mass destruction. Any ethical model that does not resonate with current modes of thought or fails to address contemporary concerns will have a hard time gaining support within Christian communities.
- **Theological fruitfulness.** The ability of a model to solve problems effectively, and to integrate doctrines that previously appeared to be

unrelated, will guarantee its support and longevity within communities.

- **Fruitfulness in enabling Christians to relate successfully to those outside their own group.** The more a moral approach makes it possible for its adherents to communicate with other Christians, and with those outside Christian communities (Jews, Muslims, Hindus, and Buddhists), the more support it will have. This ability has always been a definite strength of natural law ethics, and one of the major reasons that Richard McCormick disliked use of sectarian or specifically "Christian" approaches to medical ethics by Christian physicians or health care ethicists.

Besides these substantive criteria, there are a number of formal principles that can be used to critique any moral theory. For instance, Tom L. Beauchamp and James F. Childress provide a list of formal criteria in their widely used and frequently revised *Principles of Bio-Medical Ethics:* **Clarity, simplicity, coherence, consistency, and the ability to advance the discipline.** Further, the Harvard scientist, E.O. Wilson, has proposed an appealing additional criteria in his important work *Consilience: The Unity of Knowledge* (1998)—**consilience**, the ability of a theory or notion to "jump over" or to make connections, and in the process to tie insights together.

I will not make any effort here to critique each of the six moral models using these criteria. The task would be a burden, and would simply limit readers in their own creative judgments. Protestant and Catholic readers, liberals and conservatives, and Europeans and Asians, will obviously apply the criteria according to their own faith systems and life histories; each will see that all the models possess definite strengths, as well as obvious limitations. James Gustafson's theocentric ethics, for instance, will appeal to those who have associations with Lutheran communities, doctrines and moralities. This model will be judged to be more scriptural and more traditional than Joseph Fletcher's situation ethics. It will generate a stronger sense of corporate identity, and be seen to be more fruitful. The latter, however, will hold strong appeal (I expect) with those Christian nurses and personnel directors caught up in life's endless round of decision making, in particular, those who have some awareness of contemporary Anglo-American philosophical morality, and who live by weighing the benefits and burdens or cost-effectiveness of actions.

On the other hand, for professional Christian women who have grown up in large urban Methodist or Catholic communities, Sharon

Welch's feminist ethics will appear (I assume) to be the "best" moral model because it resonates better with their experience, it fosters admired values and virtues, and enables them to relate better to peers and family members.

* * * *

In coming years, Christian ethicists will reflect at greater length on method questions, such as, the place of women's experience or the use of the Bible in making life and death decisions in hospitals. They will build upon the last 30 years; they will be more able (perhaps) to break free from the bonds (some intellectual, others magisterial) that limit current moral research. Future theologians will be more confident in their use of the social sciences; they will be more expert in their command of biology and genetics; and they will be better equipped to assess the value of postmodernism's contributions to science, literature, human language, and knowledge. These theologians, well versed in Scripture, will be better placed than today's to respond to Bonhoeffer's paradoxical words, "The knowledge of good and evil seems to be the aim of all ethical reflection. The first task of Christian ethics is to invalidate this knowledge. In launching this attack on the underlying assumptions of all other ethics, Christian ethics stands so completely alone that it becomes questionable whether there is any purpose in speaking of Christian ethics at all."[1]

I have no doubt that Christian ethics will experience what Avery Dulles said in 1974 in bringing his *Models of the Church* to a close: "Under the leading of the Holy Spirit the images and forms of Christian life will continue to change, as they have in previous centuries. In a healthy community of faith the production of new myths and symbols goes on apace. The ecclesiologists of the future will no doubt devise new models of thinking about the Church" (192). Vatican II expressly urged theologians and pastoral leaders to undertake the revision of the Church's ethics, to strengthen its scriptural foundations, and its sense of the dignity of marriage and the life of the laity. This was a definite sign that changes had to be made, and that the "models" of morality central to the manuals used in Catholic seminaries needed to be altered by being either set aside or brought up to date.

Finally, the Church is Christ's body, and the Church is the pillar and ground of God's truth. As Gerard Manley Hopkins said so well, "The world is charged with the grandeur of God." However, nobody should presume that today's Christian ethics, as embodied in either James Gustafson's theocentric model or Sharon Welch's feminist model, is

God's best or final word. Theology, as Gustafson reminds us, contains, like Scripture, the words of God in the symbols and cultures of women and men—it is full of cultural distortions, linguistic, and sexist biases. The Church's morality must be forever reformed and renewed by prophetic thinkers and poetic voices. The limitations found in the writings of individual Christian moral authors can be found as well in the history-bound and culturally connected moral traditions of the worldwide faith communities, in the Protestant, Catholic, and Orthodox churches. This does not mean that there are not significant ethical insights ("truths") within these traditions, or that these traditions when faithfully followed, will not lead those who respect and follow them to virtue. It simply means that these traditions are never perfect, never without the limitations associated with the lasting impact of Adam's fall.

The models of Christian ethics that will emerge during this and later centuries cannot be rigid copies of old ones, whether today's or yesterday's. They must embody the prayerful effort and intellectual rigor of their creators, as well as the central thrusts toward spiritual, social, and human renewal that are found in the old ones. Nevertheless, the moral models that are still to be born in God's own time will arise from the conviction that the Church, "the people of God," is the starting point and basis of Christian ethics as it mingles with human experience of the right and the good. It takes political, social and linguistic form without becoming the manifesto of any political party.

For, as T. Ralph Morton, a member of the group of laity and clergy who went to Iona in 1938 to rebuild a monastery there that had fallen into ruins, said, "The Church can never become a political party, nor the congregation a political cell." And it cannot take these steps, because this path would "set at nought its [the Church's] primary task of being a home of reconciliation whose one sufficient weapon must be love."[2]

Whatever the date and place, the Church that was established in the world by Pentecost will witness through its moral models and lived ethics to Christ and his kingdom. It will show itself as lighthouse as well as fortress, satellite as well as evening star—God's enduring, yet ever-changing symbol of hope and the "not yet." For the Church to be *Church*, it and its ethics, must be *semper reformanda*.

NOTES

[1] Dietrich Bonhoeffer, *Ethics* (New York: MacMillan, 1955), 12.
[2] T. Ralph Morton, *Community of Faith: The Changing Pattern of the Church's Life* (New York: Association Press, 1954), 92.

INDEX